PRAYER

*Beginning
Conversations
with God*

RICHARD J. BECKMEN

Augsburg
MINNEAPOLIS

PRAYER: Beginning Conversations with God

Cover and inside design: Steven Broin, Visual Image Studio Inc.

Beckmen, Richard J.
    Prayer: beginning conversations with God/Richard J Beckmen.
        p.   cm.
    Includes bibliographical references.
    ISBN 0-8066-2768-9 (pbk.)
    1. Prayer.   I. Title.
BV215.B4 1995
242--dc20   94-42239
                                                                  CIP

The paper used in this publication meets the minimum requirements of American National Standards for Information Sciences— Permanence of Paper for Printed Library Materials, ANSI Z329.48-1984.   ∞™

Manufactured in the U.S.A.   AF 10-27689

01   02   03   04   05   4   5   6   7   8   9   10

CONTENTS

PREFACE

hat is prayer? How do I pray? Why does prayer seem so difficult sometimes? If you ask questions like these, *Prayer: Beginning Conversations with God* will be a helpful companion to you on your prayer journey. Because the book is designed to help both new and experienced pray-ers grow in their understanding and practice of prayer, each chapter concludes with questions for reflection and discussion and exercises that will help readers explore the chapter's subject further. There are more activities suggested than you will probably use. Select the ones that are most appropriate for you at this time in your prayer journey.

If you are studying with a group, the following suggestions might be of help to you.

- Include a variety of prayer experiences in your group meetings. Use silent prayer, prayer hymns, sentence prayers, and so forth.
- Encourage group members to read the section of the book you will be discussing and consider the questions and experiences at the end of the chapter.
- When your group meets, relate personal reflections as you are moved to do so. You do not have to share everything you think about or write in your journal.
- In addition to the questions and exercises in the book, discuss questions that arise from the group. Encourage group members to share personal prayer experiences related to the topic and to talk about areas of special interest.
- Avoid giving the impression that everyone ought to be in the same place

in his or her spiritual journey. Accept others where they are and seek to encourage one another.
- Do not be concerned merely to get through the book. Be attentive to the questions and struggles people in the group might have and allow for group discussion.
- Members of the group could become prayer partners for one another.

In the Book of Exodus we read, "Thus the Lord used to speak to Moses face to face, as one speaks to a friend" (Exodus 33:11). And the apostle Paul described Christian maturity by explaining, "For now we see in a mirror dimly, but then we will see face to face" (1 Corinthians 13:12). *Prayer: Beginning Conversations with God* is part of a collection of materials identified with the phrase "face to face with God." It is my prayer that this book will help you grow in your relationship with God, that you will see God face to face.

—*Richard J. Beckmen*

About the Cover

The fern is a symbol of piety because ferns grow deep in the forest, not by the highway, so they have to be sought out to be seen. The grape vine is a traditional symbol of God's identification with his people.

Chapter One

INTRODUCTION *to* PRAYER

here are many reasons you might be drawn to pray. You might feel like a victim caught in circumstances beyond your control. Lacking a sense of your own power, you might reach beyond yourself, hoping to find divine assistance.

Memories of a childhood intimacy with God now absent in the rush of a busy life might draw you to seek prayer in order to restore a relationship with God that once seemed so close and comforting. This was the situation of a man sitting next to me on the plane. He noticed I was reading a book about God. He started a conversation that soon got around to the story of his life, especially as it related to God. Before the flight was over he had shared with me the tale of his loss of intimacy with God. He no longer prayed. He was not even sure how to begin. He asked me to tell him how to recapture the close communication with God he had as a young person.

Grief, too, might kindle in you a desire to learn to pray. Perhaps the loss of a loved one through death, divorce, separation, or abandonment has pushed you to the edge. In desperation you might turn to God.

At different times in your life, an inner longing to fill a spiritual void might begin to tug at you. In whatever way God might catch our attention, people are moved to pray, or at least to begin asking the questions that can lead to prayer.

Where is the caring One who hears, listens, and responds to my needs?

Where is the One who loves me deeply so that my need for intimacy is satisfied?

Where is the One in whose presence joy erupts from my heart?

Where is the One who understands my pain and frustration?

These questions have their roots in the search for spirituality—a relationship that nurtures the deepest part of us. Each of us is at a different place on our spiritual journey. Some are just beginning or are moving on to new forms and experiences in prayer. If this is where you are, try not to compare yourself with others. Rather, pay attention to your own journey. Be aware of your needs and desires in your relationship to God and pursue the path of prayer that will allow you to continue in your spiritual growth. Even though you might find this journey difficult at times, know that it will bear fruit in your life. It is a journey to which we are all called and in which we can all discover a more complete humanity.

Of course, some people—perhaps you are among them—already have deep and meaningful prayer disciplines. They might have prayed their entire lives, or perhaps they have more recently been led to develop such a discipline. Those who have been involved in Twelve Step groups speak of discovering that the primary issue in facing and sustaining freedom from addictive behavior is their spirituality, a surrendered relationship to a power greater than themselves.

Whether you are new to prayer or are a lifelong pray-er, ultimately the act of prayer does not come from within yourself. C. G. Jung, who served as psychiatrist to many, said that all his patients ultimately were faced with spiritual issues. The great theologian Augustine exclaimed, "Our hearts are restless until they find their rest in you, O God." God is the initiator of prayer. Prayer is our response to God's invitation to be part of a loving relationship with the One who made us, sustains us, and finally saves us from ourselves and the power of sin to destroy us.

The amazing thing about prayer is that God is always there, even before we think of praying. God already calls and invites us to experience a relationship in which the divine can touch our lives. God creates the foundation of the relationship and the desire within us to enter into it. The prophet Isaiah reminds us that God is aware and responsive even before we can utter our prayer. "Before they call I will answer, while they are yet speaking I will hear" (Isaiah 65:24).

God our Creator, the One in whose image we are made, longs to communicate with us. In Jesus, God has expressed this desire by extending a grace-filled invitation of reconciling love, and through the Word and the Holy Spirit, we are encouraged to seek God's face.

What Is Prayer?

Some people think prayer is "saying a prayer"—speaking a particular intention to God. Prayer, however, can be understood more generally than that.

Prayer, in a broad sense, links all aspects of our lives to God. God is present in all of life. We might set aside certain times and places for worship, but God is not absent from any time or any place. It is right and proper to pray at all times and in all places.

Prayer is the name we give to the experience of being in communication with God, wherever we are and whatever we are doing. Prayer is experience because it involves our senses, minds, souls, and spirits. When we pray, we know that it is happening. Prayer is a point of interaction with God.

Prayer is communication because it involves giving and receiving. It is sharing between two living, personal beings—God and yourself. In all the various forms and methods of prayer, there is something going on between the person of the Christian and the person of God. You are sharing your life: your needs, feelings, concerns, and desires. God is responding with divine presence, consolation, insight, and change.

To be sure, prayer is not communication between equals. As Creator and Divine Spirit, God is far above and beyond what we can know. God has revealed in Jesus much of his heart, will, and mind. We know God's name and we know the mystery of his will in Christ Jesus to draw all persons to himself. We know God's continuing presence in the Holy Spirit and all of the ways the Holy Spirit ministers in our lives. However, we acknowledge that we do not know all there is to know about God.

This tension between knowing and not knowing about God affects our prayer life. This tension between God's otherness and our likeness to God—our creation in God's image—defines some of the struggle in prayer. God remains in control but is open to our requests and intercessions. God remains essentially hidden yet gives glimpses of his workings and will. God is holy and other from us yet dwells among us and in us through the Holy Spirit. God is distant yet near.

Our own condition adds to the dilemma created by the differences between God and ourselves. We are limited to space and time yet touched by the eternal. We are sinners, yet through Christ's redemption we are invited to the throne room of God. We stumble in darkness, yet God shares light and revelation with us. Our trust in God is tainted by shame, fear, and guilt, yet God desires that we come close to him as he has come close to us.

All of these tensions say that prayer needs to be grounded in humility but expressed in faith and hope. Most of Jesus' teaching on prayer focuses on this basic point. We are to come to God as a child to a parent, as a creature to the divine Creator, as a sinner to the Holy One. But at the same time we are to pray as a friend of God: in confidence that God hears and will respond, persistently and fervently because our prayers make a difference, in humility as the earth creatures that we are, but with all confidence and hope as the beloved children of God that we are as well.

Prayer, broadly understood, is also the way we offer all of who we are and what we do in the dialog with God. Our spirituality is a part of our body, mind, feelings, and will. It is a part of our worship, work, play, and rest. As God seeks to be always and everywhere present, so we seek to be always and everywhere present to God.

Prayer is centering our life in our relationship with God in Christ and allowing that center to be present in all we do. Christ will satisfy the hungering soul. Christ will bring solace to the pained heart. Christ will respond to the cry for mercy or the complaint for justice. Christ will be there when we simply need to feel that our relationship with God is warm and real. Christ will be there for rest, guidance, joy, love, and hope. In prayer we present our whole life and the lives of others to God, so that God may be known and lives may be touched by grace.

Does Prayer Work?

Do we experience God today as more than a spectator to our life journey?

In this book you are invited to explore various descriptions of prayer that come from the conviction that prayer is the mightiest force in the world and that it provides an avenue for a spirituality that can speak to the deepest yearnings and searchings of the human heart.

Does prayer work? First we need to define what we mean by the word *work*. If it means we can run an experiment such as we might do in a laboratory, then the answer would be no. Scientific thinking that is based on a repeatable cause-and-effect relationship will not work in relation to prayer. Such thinking assumes that we can control the mind and activity of God and ensure that God will do whatever we ask. There really is no guarantee that a prayer will be answered in the way we want it to be answered. Experiments have been done to show that, in general, prayer has an effect. However, the specific outcome requested cannot be guaranteed every time.

If by asking, "Does prayer work?" we mean, "Does God hear our prayer and answer according to his will and purpose?" the answer is yes. There is an important assumption beneath this question. The assumption has to do with who is in charge and how we understand the world and ourselves in relationship to God. Our natural inclination is to believe that our life is the center of the universe and that all others, including God, revolve around our life. Imagine the thinking of people before the time of Galileo. They believed that the sun, moon, stars, and planets revolved about the earth. Everything else, they believed, moved according to a plan that served earth. We now know that the sun is at the center of our solar system and that all else revolves around it.

Similarly, I might believe that my will, understanding, and feelings are at the center of my existence and that all else—including God—is to serve me. However, the biblical picture has God at the center with my life and the lives of others orbiting around the will and purpose of God.

Adopting this biblical way of thinking involves moving the center of your life from your own ego—that self-conscious, controlling center—to that spiritual center within yourself where God directs your life. The apostle Paul describes his own experience of this transformation in Galatians 2:19-20:

> *For through the law I died to the law, so that I might live to God. I have been crucified with Christ; and it is no longer I who live, but it is Christ who lives in me. And the life I now live in the flesh I live by faith in the Son of God, who loved me and gave himself for me.*

Effective prayer is an expression of a transformed relationship with a living and personal God.

Does prayer work? If your relationship with God is working, prayer is working. Therefore, we approach God in prayer as we would approach a person in conversation. We talk, God listens. We listen, God talks. We share, God shares. We feel, God feels. God acts, we respond. We act, God responds. God has expressed this personal nature through Jesus, who lived among us as a human being. Through the gift of the Holy Spirit who dwells within, we experience this personal nature of the God who has chosen to dwell among us in the church and in our personal lives.

For REFLECTION *and* DISCUSSION

1. What circumstances or events call you to prayer? When and how are you reminded to pray? Are you prompted from the inside or by external circumstances?

2. When do you feel closest to God? When you are alone? In a church setting? With a group? In nature? Reflect on how the setting for prayer affects your experience of prayer.

3. What experiences with prayer have strengthened your faith and enhanced your relationship with God?

4. In what ways have you been influenced by our culture to think in terms of a separation between sacred and secular in your leisure time? In your sense of ownership of things? In your religious practices? In your awareness of God's presence?

ACTIVITIES

1. Write a definition of prayer that reflects how you understand and practice prayer at the present time.

2. A prayer journal can be a helpful tool for your growth in prayer. It becomes a record of your spiritual journey. Throughout this book, suggestions will be made to use your prayer journal. (Many bookstores sell books with blank pages that are suitable.) A prayer journal can have several uses.
   A. Record prayer requests or intercessions and make a note of prayers that are answered.
   B. Develop an ongoing list of people or situations for whom you wish to pray.
   C. Record your reflections or learnings about prayer.
   D. Write any insights or experiences from your meditation times in your journal.
   E. Copy prayers that are meaningful to you and enhance your prayer life.

   You might want to have more than one prayer journal—one for intercessory prayer, one for learnings, one for special prayers, and so forth.

Chapter Two

PRAYER *and* YOUR RELATIONSHIP *to* GOD

W hat you think about God will greatly affect how and why you pray. If your God is too small you might end up thinking you have to do most things yourself. If your God is too miserly you might not have great expectations of God. If your God is too much like yourself you might feel disillusioned. If you think of God as a salesperson you might end up always trying to bargain with God. If your God is angry you will probably try to hide out. None of these images provides a positive or accurate picture of God.

In John 15 Jesus describes the nature of the relationship between God and the believer: it is initiated, sustained, and interpreted through the person of Jesus. This is a critical issue for Christians. Our relationship to God is mediated through Jesus Christ. That is, we understand who God is through the teachings and actions of Jesus.

We can learn what Jesus taught about prayer and relationship from two passages. Read John 15:1-11 and notice the way prayer is linked to a relationship with Christ.

I am the true vine, and my Father is the vinegrower. He removes every branch in me that bears no fruit. Every branch that bears fruit he prunes to make it bear more fruit. You have already been cleansed by the word that I have spoken to you. Abide in me as I abide in you. Just as the branch cannot bear fruit by itself unless it abides in the vine, neither can you unless you abide in me. I am the vine, you are the branches. Those who abide in me and I in them bear much fruit, because apart from me you can do nothing. Whoever does not abide in me is thrown away like a branch and withers; such branches are gathered, thrown into the fire, and burned. If you abide in me, and my words abide in you, ask for whatever you wish, and it will be done for you. My Father is glorified by this, that you bear much fruit and become my disciples. As the Father has loved me, so I have loved you; abide in my love. If you keep my commandments, you will abide in my love, just as I have kept my Father's commandments and abide in his love. I have said these things to you so that my joy may be in you, and that your joy may be complete.

Jesus describes several aspects of the relationship. First, the image of the vine and branches indicates the relationship is organic. It is alive, real, and interdependent. The branches cannot live without nourishment from the vine. The vine depends on the branches to bear fruit. Secondly, the word *abide* conveys a sense of intimacy in the relationship. It denotes being at home or dwelling within. In addition, the relationship is marked by love, obedience, and discipline.

Out of this kind of relationship with Christ, your prayer will flow naturally and comfortably. To pray is not foreign or alien to your life as a Christian. Prayer is the way you respond to this mutual abiding: you in Christ and Christ's word in you (v. 7). This relationship allows you freedom to request of God what you wish. And because of this relationship with Christ you will know how and for what to pray.

In John's Gospel, Jesus continues his teaching about the relationship that allows us to pray with confidence and without fear:

This is my commandment, that you love one another as I have loved you. No one has greater love than this, to lay down one's life for one's friends. You are my friends if you do what I command you. I do not call you servants any longer, because the servant does not know what the master is doing; but I have called you friends, because I have made known to you everything that I have heard from my Father. You did not choose me but I chose you. And I appointed you to go and bear fruit, fruit that will last, so that the Father will give you whatever you ask him in my name. (John 15:12-16)

When you pray out of this type of relationship with Christ, you are not standing on the outside looking in. You are on the inside, sharing in the love and friendship of Christ as a child of God. Notice in these verses how Christ includes you as a friend in the inner circle of knowledge and the inner circle of his love. Notice, also, how you have been chosen and appointed to bear fruit. You belong.

This might be difficult for you to accept. Grace is difficult to accept. You might be conscious of your shortcomings and feel quite inadequate to claim such stature before God. Yet, there it is. In Christ you are a chosen, loved, and sent child of God. And because you are in Christ, you can ask whatever you will in Jesus' name (v. 16). When Christians pray in Jesus' name, we do not use Jesus' name as some sort of magical phrase like "Open, Sesame!" We use it because our relationship with God has been established through Jesus Christ and rests on our continuing relationship to him.

God has closed the distance between himself and you in Christ. In Christ God has claimed you as a child. As a child of God in Christ, you have a child's rights and privileges from a parent. This means you do not have to talk God into loving you or hearing your prayer. You do not have to bargain with God in prayer, haggling as if you were dealing with a merchant in the marketplace. You simply ask because of the kind of relationship you now have with God in Jesus Christ. Jesus' name and your willingness to identify with it provide the basis for your prayer.

Prayer and the Holy Spirit

The substance of your relationship with God, as described above, is provided by Jesus Christ. In Christ, God's love, grace, and desire to draw you near are made possible. The Holy Spirit, on the other hand, is the energy of your relationship with God. The Holy Spirit is the dynamic presence of God given to you so you can know and trust the relationship that God establishes with you in Christ. The Holy Spirit is the "present tense" of God. The Spirit makes real in your life what Jesus spoke long ago. The Holy Spirit brings Jesus' teaching and work into the present moment.

Jesus promised an intimate relationship with God based upon his death and resurrection. This relationship is established in baptism and continues to be lived out in faith (Romans 6:3-4). The Holy Spirit, given in baptism, is God's continuing presence at work through all of your life's ages and stages.

The apostle Paul describes the role of the Holy Spirit in sustaining your relationship as God's child:

> *For all who are led by the Spirit of God are children of God. For you did not receive a spirit of slavery to fall back into fear, but you have received a spirit of adoption. When we cry, "Abba! Father!" it is that very Spirit bearing witness with our spirit that we are children of God.* (Romans 8:14-16)

Paul also warns not to "grieve the Spirit" (Ephesians 4:30) or "quench the Spirit" (1 Thessalonians 5:19). To do either of these is to hinder the Spirit's work of nurturing you in the new life. If you distance yourself from the Spirit through neglect or resistance, your relationship with God will be only something remembered from the past but not experienced now. And if you ignore the Spirit, your prayer life will suffer along with other aspects of your faith life. In a stirring passage about maintaining a strong spiritual life in the face of spiritual enemies, Paul includes constant prayer in the Spirit as one of the components necessary to ensure survival (Ephesians 6:10-18).

When you are neither able nor conscious of what you should pray about, the Holy Spirit is present in you to pray. A very comforting passage from Paul describes how the Spirit will pray in you even when all you can do is groan:

> *Likewise the Spirit helps us in our weakness; for we do not know how to pray as we ought, but that very Spirit intercedes with sighs too deep for words. And God, who searches the heart, knows what is the mind of the Spirit, because the Spirit intercedes for the saints according to the will of God.*
>
> *(Romans 8:26-27)*

The Holy Spirit is God present in you and for you. The Spirit helps you to do today what God has always done: bring the kingdom of God to the lives of God's people. God, through the Spirit, will do for you what you cannot do for yourself. In many situations in life, you might not know how or for what to pray. You might not be able to discern God's will and purpose in a given situation, but God through the Spirit will pray the prayer that needs to be prayed.

This deep experience of prayer takes place within your very center. You will encounter these prayer opportunities whenever you face moments of profound grief, despair, pain, or addiction. Surrender them to the Spirit within so that the prayers that need to be prayed will be prayed.

The Holy Spirit is involved in another similar type of prayer. Many Christians experience praying in the Spirit or praying in tongues, as it is sometimes called. Praying in tongues is a nonrational experience of prayer. The prayer does not consciously control what is being said. In fact, the one praying is not using a language he or she knows. This prayer, prayed by the Spirit through the person who has surrendered conscious control, edifies the spirit of the person praying. That is, it upbuilds and strengthens the spiritual dimension of the person: relationship with God, joy in God's presence, and spiritual understanding.

Praying in the Spirit is a manifestation of the Spirit's presence and is one of many spiritual gifts given by God through the Spirit for the ministry and mission of the church. You can request this gift from God through prayer. Pray also for wisdom, humility, and, most of all, love. All spiritual gifts are dangerous if directed by a proud and possessive ego. Praying in the Spirit, like other spiritual gifts, is meant to be a blessing to you and others under the direction of God's love. (Read 1 Corinthians 14 and Acts 19:1-7 to explore more fully how the Bible describes this form of prayer and its use.)

As you might expect, all three persons of the Trinity are involved in your prayer life as they are involved in your faith relationship to God. Each person of the Trinity may be addressed in prayer. Each person of the Trinity is involved in the response to your prayer. There is no end to the excitement and adventure this kind of relationship holds for you, especially for your prayer life.

For REFLECTION *and* DISCUSSION

1. Describe the mental images that you have of God. What feelings about God do you associate with these images? How do these images and feelings affect your sense of your relationship with God?

2. Think about a close relationship you have with another person. Compare that relationship with your relationship with God. How are they similar? How are they different?

3. What part does feeling play in your relationship with God through Jesus Christ?

4. What role does Jesus play in defining your relationship to God? Is the image in John's Gospel of the vine and branches descriptive of your relationship with God and Jesus? What is your favorite image for describing your relationship with God?

5. What role does the Holy Spirit play in your prayer life? In what ways are you conscious of the Holy Spirit being active in you?

ACTIVITIES

1. Spend time reflecting on the following scripture passages that describe various aspects of the believer's relationship to God. In your reflection, seek to understand your own response to each passage. Do you feel confused? Does

the passage describe any of your own experiences? Are there any statements that cause you to resist or draw back? Are there images or experiences described that draw you to explore more deeply? Choose one passage for each day and live with it, taking time during the day to reflect on it in relation to your own life and experience.

Isaiah 43:1-2
Romans 8:1-4
Matthew 11:28
John 3:16-17
Ephesians 2:4-10

2. Take a walk outside. As you walk allow yourself to become absorbed in the thought that all that you see is a gift from God. Let all your senses be alive and open to the realization of God's grace coming to you through creation. Write in your journal about your responses to the walk.

3. Read Luke 10:38-42. The story of Mary and Martha reflects two different ways to show hospitality and welcome to Jesus. One is focused on the outer hospitality and the other on the inner. Do you see yourself in one of these more than the other? Do you desire to be more like one than the other? What do you think it would take to accomplish this? Write in your journal about your responses to this passage and to each of the characters in the story.

4. In order to enhance your daily sense of God's presence, choose an object that you can carry with you at all times. It will serve as a reminder to be conscious of God and stimulate you to pray. It could be small stone, a cross, a certain bracelet, or some other small object. Write a brief prayer that helps you celebrate God's presence. Use it regularly.

5. Experiment for one week with a daily discipline of praying specifically at set times during the day. Try scheduling five different times during the day when you consciously stop what you are doing and engage in a prayer: on awakening, at meal times, and before bed might be a practical schedule. Each prayer time could focus on a different prayer concern or could use a different prayer style.

Chapter Three

PRAYER LANGUAGE *and* POSTURE

*P*rayer and Language

When we pray to God, to whom are we praying? What images do we use in prayer? What experiences and information have formed the images that dictate what words we use? The answers to these questions help us understand the way we pray.

Our images of God and the language we use in prayer might come from several sources. One is the experience we have in worship. Styles of prayer in public worship often convey the way people think they ought to pray. Another source might be the prayer experiences of childhood—listening to the prayers of a parent at mealtime or bedtime.

The Bible provides, for most people, the images and often the language of prayer. Whole generations can be nurtured on a particular Bible translation that will shape their understanding of God and the language they think should be used in prayer. As an example, for years the King James Version was the primary translation used in the English-speaking world. God was addressed as "thee" and "thou." In more recent times, as translations have changed the language used to address God in the Bible, many people find themselves addressing God as "you" and speaking to God in the same way they might speak to a neighbor or friend, using the common language spoken between humans.

Using a distinct language for God—"thee" and "thou," for instance—stresses God's transcendence. Such language conveys the sense that communication with God is different from communication with another human, and that a relationship with God is different from any other relationship a person has.

On the other hand, to use the same language for prayer as that used in every other relationship stresses closeness and familiarity with God. It emphasizes the immanence of God—the presence of God within and among us. Jesus, on occasion, used the word *abba* to address God in prayer. This is an Aramaic word that most Bible translators interpret as "father." However, in English the word carries much more the sense of "daddy" or "papa." Abba is obviously a very informal and intimate term for God.

Another source of imagery for understanding God is our experience. Personal spiritual experiences of God might provide images that influence how we think of God and address God. People who have shared these experiences report that some of them have created a deep sense of awe and otherness of God, while other people have discovered an intimate nearness and informality in God's presence.

Another concern in the area of prayer and language is the role of feminine and masculine metaphors for God in shaping our images and prayer language. With the rise of feminine consciousness, our traditions have been revisited in the light of this new awareness. The predominant images of God in our Western culture and church make use of what we traditionally have named masculine characteristics. These images have shaped much of the thinking and praying of the church. Traditionally the pronoun "he" has been used almost exclusively with reference to God. The use of such language and images has tended to create the idea that God is totally male.

However, the Bible teaches that God is spirit—neither male nor female. Yet for us to speak about God or to God, we have to use language related to our experience and learning. When we speak of someone, we imagine a person with certain characteristics and qualities that are either masculine or feminine. The same is true of God. The Scriptures contain metaphors for God that are labeled masculine or feminine; that is, that tend to be identified with men or women. We do not have any other way to understand a personal being.

Because our tradition is patriarchal, the masculine "God as Father" has dominated our image and language for God. "Mother" is not a name most Christians would apply to God, even though the Bible contains many mothering metaphors. But many women and men today are seeking to express the fullness of God by making the language of worship and prayer more inclusive of feminine images and language. It is a difficult struggle. However, as we pay more attention to the Bible's feminine images of God, we will be able to see the fullness of God expressed in all sorts of ways that cover the full range of human need, and we will be able to use these long-neglected images of God and will find ourselves free to use inclusive language.

There is a name God used in the Bible that is not related to a specific activity and, therefore, appears to be free from gender identification. When Moses was confronted by God through the burning bush, Moses asked God's name. God replied with the name "I Am"—a name that is all-inclusive of being and of time and of the very ground of being. We can create an image of the activity of God—I Am—in the lives of people and in creation by looking at all the ways we act as men and women. God has been described in the Bible as warrior, judge, father (Deuteronomy 1:31), comforting mother (Isaiah 66:13), and in many other ways. It is important to remember that these metaphors for God describe relationships and not the essence or nature of God.

Jesus tells two parables in Luke 15 that use both masculine and feminine metaphors for God. They are the parables about the shepherd who leaves ninety-nine sheep to find the one separated from the flock, and the woman who has ten coins but loses one of them and searches diligently until she finds it. The same truth is being expressed in two different stories. In one God is pictured as a shepherd. In the other God is pictured as a woman in search of her lost coin.

If you were to compose prayers based on these two parables and their message of God reaching out to the lost, they could read something like this:

O God, Shepherd of the world, thank you for diligently risking all to find me and carry me back to the fold of your people. Amen.

O God, Woman of patient compassion, thank you for your willingness to look in the dark corners of the world to save your lost ones. Thank you for your diligent search for me when I hide beneath the dust under the bed. Amen.

We do not have to choose between masculine or feminine images and language for God. We can embrace both—along with many other images—so that the fullness of God's revelation can be experienced. Out of that experience we can begin to expand our understanding of God and gain courage to express, in the language of our prayers, a full awareness of the wonder and mystery of God. At the same time, using both images will give women and men the knowledge and experience that they are created equally in the image of God, inasmuch as God is willing to be among us in both masculine and feminine activity.

For men, allowing the feminine metaphors equal footing with the masculine might create tension and discomfort, but growth usually involves such discomfort. Explore this area of prayer so that your devotional life can be enriched by a broader awareness of God's activity. You will probably discover parts of yourself that you will express more easily in prayer as you acknowledge and allow expression of the feminine within you. This can be a liberating experience and help you find wholeness as a man.

For women, this exploration in broadening the images and language of prayer can be liberating as well. Because masculine metaphors have dominated so much of religious expression, discovering the feminine in images and language for prayer will affirm who you are and free you from relying only on masculine metaphors in your devotional expression. This might be particularly helpful if you have been victimized or felt put down as a woman within the religious community, in your family, or in the community at large.

It is important for you to find your language and voice in prayer. Let your prayer be yours. You have a relationship with God, and God desires to hear what you think, feel, experience, and desire. As you read the Bible and reflect on the God you have experienced in Jesus Christ and your community of faith, let the images create a language that for you will release gratitude, praise, concern, and compassion.

Prayer and the Body

What does the body have to do with prayer? I was a student intern from seminary serving a church in North Dakota. It was Lent and I was presiding at my first Holy Communion service at this church. When it came time in the service for the prayer of confession, I turned to the altar, knelt, and began to pray the long confessional prayer. When the prayer was done, I stood up and turned to announce the words of forgiveness. I was shocked. Everybody had left the church! My eyes quickly surveyed the whole sanctuary and everyone was gone. Some seconds went by as I stood there in silence. Then I noticed the top of one head slowly rising to eye level from behind a pew. Suddenly I knew what had happened. Everyone, from the youngest to the oldest, was kneeling on the floor with their folded hands and heads resting on the seats of the pew. I spoke the words of forgiveness, the people stood, and the service went on. I had never seen this before, but it was a long-standing tradition in this congregation. Confessing was an act of the body as well as the mind, will, and emotions.

People of all religions use particular forms of body posture in prayer. In fact, in some religions certain postures are required for prayer. Five times a day a devout Muslim will kneel and face Mecca to pray. Yoga as a prayer discipline focuses on body positions.

Some Christians kneel to pray. Others stand. Still others sit. Some bow their heads. Some look out and around. Different types of prayer might call for different postures.

You might experience something through your body that does not come through your mind or feelings. You might express a deeper sense of humility by kneeling. You might experience a sense of total commitment or adoration by lying prostrate on the floor. Standing might give you a sense of being uplifted, while sitting might provide a more comfortable, focused position for a long period of prayer.

When you were a child you were probably taught to fold your hands when you prayed. This was probably to keep you from being distracted by playing with things around you. Prayer is a focused activity, and being distracted by thinking or doing things not connected with prayer hinders your concentration. But you can do other things with your hands when you pray. Especially in Asia, placing the hands together and holding them in front of the body is a sign of respect and honor, and this posture is used by Asians and others in prayer. Some people raise their hands as a sign for blessing God with praise. This was a practice among the Old Testament pray-ers, as seen in Psalm 134:2: "Lift up your hands to the holy place, and bless the Lord."

Praying with hands open to God is a symbol that can have a powerful effect on the attitude of prayer. Often we approach God with our hands clenched tightly around our needs, fears, or possessions. We come to talk with God but continue to try to keep some things hidden. To show hands open and empty reveals to God that we have given up our attachments. We extend our hands, ready to receive what God will give.

In his book *With Open Hands*, Henri J.M. Nouwen notes: "The resistance to praying is like the resistance of tightly clenched fists. This image shows the tension, the desire to cling tightly to yourself, a greediness which betrays fear."

Sometimes the body can lead the heart to a place of openness and receptivity toward God. Lifting open hands extended out toward God, you might find your heart more willing to surrender to God. Kneeling might, as well, encourage your spirit to bend in honest humility. If you make your body still and close your eyes, embracing silence, your soul might see itself in a new way.

In many cultures, dance is part of the prayer experience. In dance the body is allowed to give full expression to what the pray-er feels toward God and desires to receive from God. When God liberated the people of Israel from Egypt and led them safely across the Red Sea, their response was singing and dancing to express their joy and thanksgiving (Exod. 15:20-21).

In mainline Christian denominations in Europe and the United States, dance became separated from religious worship. Dance was categorized as secular activity. Emotions and ecstasy in the church were something to be avoided. It became important to sit still, kneel still, and stand still. In many churches, excessive movement is suspect. However, a renewal of liturgical dance is bringing this form of prayer back into the church.

The open hand, the uplifted arms, the body moving in freedom to express adoration, gratitude, confession, and pleading—all of these point to ways the body can join with the heart, mind, and spirit in the conversation we call prayer. You have only to observe a person signing hymns and prayers for the hearing impaired to begin to appreciate the ways the body can participate in prayer.

For REFLECTION *and* DISCUSSION

1. Reflect on the source of your primary images of God. What passages of Scripture have influenced that image? How has language shaped your image of God?

2. Can you think of scripture references that use feminine images or metaphors for God's activity? How comfortable are you when you think about God having feminine characteristics?

3. When you address God in prayer, are you more comfortable with formal or informal language? Why?

4. How do you feel when you hear others addressing God in a way different from what you are used to?

5. How would you describe the relationship of your body to your prayer activity? Not involved? Participating? A hindrance? An asset?

ACTIVITIES

1. Practice writing prayers that respond to both the feminine and masculine characteristics of God's activity.

2. Many names or titles for Jesus are based on what he does or has done. Write down as many names or titles for Jesus as you can think of that come from the New Testament. List the activity or characteristic they describe. Are there names or titles you can give to Jesus that are based on your own experience of what he has done or what he means to you? Write these down also.

3. Experiment with various body postures as you pray. Sit. Kneel. Stand. Lie down on the floor. What postures feel appropriate for you to use? Are any of them emotionally uncomfortable for you? Are some types of prayer suited to certain postures?

4. Experiment with different hand positions in prayer: folded, hands extended with palms up, and hands raised over the head. What do you learn about prayer from these various hand positions? What do you learn about your own responses to them?

5. Experiment with using dance in your personal prayers. Play a tape of liturgical music or a hymn and let your body respond with a prayer dance. Let your body pick up the theme of the music and express thanks, praise, pain, concern, joy, or sorrow. Let your heart, mind, and spirit follow your body in this prayer. Write in your journal about your feelings and responses to this physical way of praying.

6. Explore the possibility of a special place in your home for a prayer center. It could be a chair or a special room. A prayer center could be created with a table on which candles, a cross, or an icon is placed. Items from nature, such as flowers, a rock, or a branch could be placed there also.

1. Henri J. M. Nouwen, *With Open Hands* (Notre Dame, Ind.: Ave Maria Press, 1972), p. 12.

Chapter Four

FACING OBSTACLES *to* PRAYER

rayer is not without its struggles. Prayer can become difficult because we lack knowledge, or because of our own inner attitudes or our failure to follow specific principles of spiritual discipline. In your prayer journey you will probably encounter most of these obstacles. Even those who are considered giants in the disciplines of prayer and spirituality share how they have struggled. No one is immune from questions and problems related to prayer.

Why Don't I Pray?

This question might be a shortened version of a whole host of similar questions: "Why don't I pray like Mr. Smith or Mrs. Jones?" "Why don't I pray except in crises?" "Why don't I feel like praying as much as I think I should?"

Such questions suggest several issues. One issue is the struggle with what the church calls the enemies of spiritual life—the devil, the world, and our own sinful selves. Just as prayer is centered in a relationship with a personal God, so overcoming the inertia to pray involves struggling with the enemies of that relationship. The tendency to try to live without God is always present in us. This tendency can be fed by guilt. If you have not been praying as you think you should, you might think God is angry and be afraid to come to God. Such guilt and fear can easily quench the desire to pray. Recalling God's forgiving grace and responding to the image of Jesus standing at the door, gently knocking, might encourage you to pray.

The experience of grace nurtures the desire to pray. This is why the daily practice of confession and forgiveness is so important. It will keep you centered in God's love and provide an environment where the Holy Spirit stirs your desire to pray in response to this experience of love. Think about the experience many farm families had with their hand water pump. Until they primed it with a little water, they could not draw a full stream of water from the pump. Prayer will not flow easily from your life without the priming action of the Holy Spirit.

In addition to our own tendency to go about life without God, we encounter forces of evil that actively fight against the purposes of God in the world and our life. These forces would like nothing better than for you not to pray . Ask God to deliver and protect you from the unbelieving world and the evil one. A sign of the presence of evil in the world—and a sign of the spirit of our age in particular—is the value placed on busyness. Many think stopping to pray is a worthless way to spend time. Profits and praise are given to the busy, active person. Taking time for prayer is standing against the spirit of this age. A strong note of warning and encouragement is found in 1 Peter 5:8: "Discipline yourselves, keep alert. Like a roaring lion your adversary the devil prowls around, looking for someone to devour."

Another way to find help overcome apathy in prayer is to pray with others. It might help you to find a prayer partner—one with whom you meet regularly to pray and discuss prayer. You might meet formally with someone who serves as your spiritual director, or you might meet with a friend to share this prayer time. Your prayer companion and you will encourage and strengthen each other.

The Way I Pray Doesn't Feel Right

This obstacle might arise when you have learned to pray in a way that does not fit who you are. Most of us have learned to pray from the example of others, and they had a particular way of praying. It is possible that this person's way just might not fit you. Temperaments vary and each person prefers to perceive and express information in different ways.

In recent years, considerable study in prayer and temperament types has been carried out. Based on your personal preferences for perceiving or judging information, whether you are centered in thinking or feeling functions, or whether you prefer to get information through your senses or intuition, you will find some styles of prayer more natural for you. Differences in temperament, as well as other individual traits, suggest that you might experiment with various prayer forms. (See "For Further Reading" on page 79.)

It is important to find your own way in prayer so that it will be a natural and honest expression of who you are. Then you will feel free to focus on the particular prayer ministry to which God is calling you.

I Don't Know How to Pray on My Own

If you learned to pray as a child, you probably were dependent on others to teach you how to pray. Perhaps you memorized prayers given to you by adults, or in other ways identified with the prayer modeled by your parents, Sunday school teachers, and pastors. We learn from others not only prayer, but most other activities of the religious life as well.

Each of us needs eventually to come into ownership of our own ways to relate to God. However, many adults do not develop their own moral and spiritual understanding and practice and remain dependent on others. If this is the case for you, take up the challenge to move beyond dependency on others and on external religious practices to express your relationship to God. You are called to take the steps to own your faith and prayer life. This involves developing inner authority, taking responsibility for trust, sharing yourself with God in prayer, and making your own commitments.

Some people have given up on Christianity and the church because it seemed oppressive or failed them in a crisis. They have taken on adult responsibilities and problems but have failed at the same time to move toward an adult faith and spiritual discipline. It is no wonder that such people find their spirituality inadequate. If the church or Christian parents have genuinely failed you, however, the point is not for you to fix blame, but for you to move on to develop a mature faith. Childhood faith and experience are important and appropriate. When you become an adult, however, childlike trust should remain, but personal, adult ownership of prayer should also be present.

The important thing is to begin praying. Share your thoughts, concerns, and requests with God. Speak to God as you would to any other person. You might find it helpful to begin by speaking your prayers aloud, rather than silently thinking them.

Why Don't I Feel Anything?

You will discover dry times in your prayer life. In the rhythm of the spiritual life the desert has its place. When you pray you might feel as if nothing is happening. The important thing is not to give up in those times. The good feelings of prayer will return. Be careful at this point not to succumb to the thought that prayer has to be felt to be effective or meaningful. Primarily, you pray out of a foundation of faith and obedience. Secondarily, you pray out of emotion. After a few experiences of praying through the dry times, you begin to realize that the vibrant and creative times will return.

It is not unusual for prayer to have a rhythm, as do so many aspects of life. Those times when you feel flat and totally unexcited about prayer might be periods of incubation. They might also be times for adjustments in your inner life. Then again, dry times might be the prelude to an exciting leap of awareness or new spiritual consciousness. I and other people of prayer have had all of these experiences following times of seemingly lifeless prayer.

It has also been my experience that new Christians or newly awakened Christians are blessed by God with quick and direct answers to prayer, as if God is encouraging them in their newfound or renewed faith. But after a time, answers come more slowly and the new pray-ers find other lessons to learn.

Why Don't I Get an Answer?

The question of unanswered prayer often comes up. We can speculate about the answer to this question, but in the end it might not be possible to provide a neat solution. God invites and encourages us to pray. God promises to hear and answer our prayers. However, what we pray for does not always happen.

There are several clues about why it seems God does not answer some of our prayers. The matter of timing is important. Prayers are not always answered immediately. We might expect an immediate answer, but some circumstances needed to bring about the answer might not be in place. Many times our prayers are answered through the agency of other people and events around us. Such natural processes take time to unfold. The best answer to your prayer might take time to arrange. God has always worked through history and the processes of nature and community. The apostle Paul even reminds us that Jesus was sent in the "fullness of time," that is, when everything was ready (Galatians 4:4).

Another reason it might seem that our prayers have not been answered is that we might not be ready to hear the answer. Poet Rainer Maria Rilke reminds us that we often have to live with the question until we are ready to live with the answer. The same can be true of your prayer. Are you ready to live with what you ask for? God's delay in answering might be intended to allow you to prepare to live with the answer.

If you think God has not answered your prayers, consider also the possibility that what God has in store for you might be different from what you asked. It might be better or just different. Often God's answer is a surprise. Keep your eyes open to what is happening and realize that the answer might be there in a form you did not expect.

I once visited a church camp. While I was there, a man with whom I was talking asked that I pray for him. He had been feeling very anxious and unable to sleep. He wanted me to pray that God would heal this condition and give him back his serenity and sense of peace. I began to pray with him but sensed that I did not have the whole story. I asked him about recent events in his life. He told me that God had blessed him in a wonderful way through a large sum of money. The government had made a mistake in a payment and sent him several thousand dollars too much. He looked upon this as a blessing from God and did not report the mistake. He intended to use the money and seemed overjoyed at his windfall. In his own mind he did not see this situation as a conflict that could cause anxiety and sleeplessness. After hearing this part of the man's story, I felt ready to pray with him, but my prayer was much different from the one he was expecting. His eyes were opened to the moral conflict he was feeling in his unconscious mind. He promised to pay back the money. And if he did, I am sure his anxiety left and sleep returned.

I am surprised at how our conscious mind will not see the truth in front of us. It is easy to become blind to what is really happening and focus our prayers on the wrong thing. This man's request for prayer became an opportunity for his prayer to be answered in truth. God's answer was a surprise. And with the help of some Christian friends, he was able to face and live with that answer.

Another matter related to unanswered prayer is a key virtue of the Christian, waiting on the Lord. Patience is one of the expressions of the fruit of the Spirit (Galatians 5:22). When you pray, perhaps continuously, you are not to give up too soon. If the desire of the prayer is still with you, continue to pray. No one really knows how long God will take to answer any prayer.

The prophet Isaiah brought this word of the Lord to the people of Israel:

Why do you say, O Jacob, and speak, O Israel,
"My way is hidden from the Lord,
*   and my right is disregarded by my God"?...*
Those who wait for the Lord shall renew their strength,
*   they shall mount up with wings like eagles.*
*   (Isaiah 40:27, 31a)*

For seventy years the people of Israel prayed for an end to the exile. Finally, it came.

Another reason it might seem that your prayer has not been answered is that you might not be praying in accordance with God's will. Your first prayer can be that God will show you the prayer you are to pray.

Whenever you think your prayer has not been answered, keep focused on your relationship with God and affirm that God is for you and will work on your behalf, even if the outcome is not what you want. Learn to live with the truth expressed in Romans 8:28: "We know that all things work together for good for those who love God, who are called according to his purpose." You cannot see around the corner and do not know the future. But you can trust that God will be at work in every situation to redeem and transform it.

There are no guarantees that your life will be spared difficulty, hardship, tragedy, or disease. We cannot control everything around us. God does not choose to control everything that happens in the world, though God might intervene at times. However, God can redeem every situation. Through God's people, who operate with God's compassion and offer gifts of grace through the Spirit and good will, God wants to transform every community, family, nation, and person. In the meantime, offer your needs to God and trust God's steadfast love and promise to hear and answer your prayer, knowing that you are not abandoned in this world.

Am I Expecting Enough from God?

What are the limits of prayer? How far dare we go in making requests of God? Do our expectations influence prayer? These questions probe an area of prayer over which there is much discussion and not a little controversy. Here we explore the fine line between God's ultimate control over answers to prayer and our capacity to influence God by our prayers. Facing such paradoxes can either leave us with a sense of futility or motivate us to explore and test the limits.

Numerous biblical references encourage us to raise our expectations. They imply that we usually aim too low, either in motivation or expectation. The Letter of James encourages us to ask but cautions us to examine our motives. We are not to pray out of covetousness, greed, or deceit.

> *You do not have, because you do not ask. You ask and do not receive, because you ask wrongly, in order to spend what you get on your pleasures.*
>
> *(James 4:2-3)*

In the Letter to the Ephesians, the apostle Paul describes the capacity of God to give far more than we can ask or imagine.

> *Now to him who by the power at work within us is able to accomplish abundantly far more than all we can ask or imagine, to him be glory in the church and in Christ Jesus to all generations, forever and ever. Amen.*
>
> *(Ephesians 3:20-21)*

In the Sermon on the Mount Jesus teaches that God knows our needs.

But whenever you pray, go into your room and shut the door and pray to your Father who is in secret; and your Father who sees in secret will reward you...Your Father knows what you need before you ask him.

(Matthew 6:6, 8)

Jesus encourages us to be bold in prayer and to have high expectations in our asking: "Whatever you ask for in prayer with faith, you will receive" (Matthew 21:22).

Praying in accordance with God's will and rooted in faith, we are encouraged to ask for whatever we will. God is ready and willing to be the loving parent blessing the child who comes in trust and obedience.

Do I Remember to Say Thank You?

When we read the story of Jesus healing ten lepers, the ending comes as something of a shock. They are cured on their way to show themselves to the priest. However, only one returns to Jesus when he sees that he is made well. Jesus' question when this man returns is the question we could all ask: "Where are the other nine?"

It is hard to imagine experiencing that kind of healing and then failing to return to give thanks. Yet that is not so unusual. We seem to have a difficult time remembering the giver of our blessings. Remember that when you pray and receive an answer, the prayer is not complete until you have given thanks. In the act of gratitude, the blessing becomes more complete. You complete the circle by acknowledging the One who answered.

Jesus' response to the one leper who returns to give thanks is to declare that he has not only been cured but made whole. His healing has become part of his relationship with Jesus, and by returning and giving thanks he has been brought into a deeper relationship with him.

I have seen this deepening occur when people come to our church's Sunday evening healing service. On occasion, individuals who have experienced healing will come back to offer prayers of thanksgiving to God for their healing. In that act I sense a deeper healing taking place within them—their relationship with God grows stronger and they find a great joy in God's activity in their lives.

Giving thanks is a great antidote to bitterness and cynicism. It is hard to give thanks and still maintain a mean or bitter spirit. Each day, find ways to give thanks in prayer so that it becomes a natural way to act. Pray at meal times.

At the end of the day remember the ways God has blessed you. Recall the specific prayers God has answered for you and offer thanks for them. Gratitude for answered prayer nurtures the spirit of prayer in your life. If you continually acknowledge God as the giver of all good gifts in your life and the One who answers prayer, you will live with a much greater awareness of God's presence and grace in your life.

For REFLECTION *and* DISCUSSION

1. Which of the obstacles described in this chapter apply to your prayer life? How have you responded to these obstacles?

2. If your prayer experience is limited, reflect on the reasons you have not been praying consistently. Does it have to do with your understanding of God? Does it relate to your lack of awareness about prayer and its possibilities? Have you had negative experiences with prayer?

3. What obstacles to a vital prayer life have you encountered that are not listed in this chapter? What ways have you discovered to overcome them?

4. Have any obstacles become insurmountable to you? Examine the causes within yourself and the circumstances around you. Is there a particular situation that seems to be commonly present when this obstacle appears? Is there an ongoing, compulsive area of your life that is blocking effective prayer?

5. Our personalities influence how we pray and the ways of praying that we find fulfilling. Is the way you are praying satisfying to you? Have you been influenced by others to pray a certain way that does not seem natural to you? How might you pray differently so that your prayer life will reflect more of who you are?

ACTIVITIES

1. Use a concordance to look up scripture references on *prayer*. Make notes on what you learn from each passage about prayer. Set aside a portion of your prayer journal for this exercise so the material will be organized for future use. Notice particularly how these scripture passages might help you overcome obstacles or answer problems you might be facing.

2. Keep track of the rhythm of your spiritual awareness and energy. Notice when you are up and when you are down. Think about the effect of this rhythm on your prayer life. Makes notes in your journal on the ebb and flow of your prayer life.

3. If there are many obstacles in your prayer life or if your spiritual journey seems blocked at this point, it might be important for you to find someone to talk to. Seek out a spiritual director or spiritual friend who can help you reflect on your situation, ask questions that might get you moving, and listen together with you for clues about what God might be doing in your inner life.

4. During the next few days, practice making an inventory at the end of each day. Later you can do this periodically, especially when you are facing difficulties in prayer. In your evening inventory, recount the ways God has blessed you during the day; remember hurts and resentments that occurred that day; note the mood that dominated your day and examine its causes; be aware of any unfinished tasks that are weighing upon you. Finish your inventory with a prayer period that relates to all of these areas. Give thanks. Ask for and give forgiveness. Pray through the issues affecting your dominant mood. Turn over the unfinished tasks to tomorrow and let the day end in God's gracious care.

5. Sometimes your prayer life might seem to be bogged down because you are praying only one kind of prayer—the same prayer over and over. Use a simple formula to broaden your prayer experience. Some people use this pattern:

    Adoration: Praise God for who God is.

    Confession: Confess your known sins to God and ask God to forgive them. Then ask God to cleanse you from sins of which you are not aware.

    Thanksgiving: Call to mind the blessings of the day and express gratitude to God for them.

    Supplication: Pray for your own needs and the needs of others.

    Experiment with this pattern and notice if it has a positive affect on your prayers.

Chapter Five

PRAYER *as* REQUEST

The first steps in prayer are often taken as a cry of desperation. Things have gotten out of hand. The world is pressing in. A terrible disaster hits. Sickness comes. Life makes no sense. You come to God asking for a change. Rescue me. Heal me. Change my partner. Forgive my sins. Give me courage. Help me pass this test. Is such prayer appropriate?

If your life were yours alone to figure out and handle, then such prayer would not be appropriate. But you have not been created by God and then abandoned to manage by yourself. God clearly desires to be a part of your life.

When our first parents in the garden of Eden broke the relationship with God and began to suffer the consequences of their rebellion, God appeared and held out to them a promise to be at work to save them. When the descendants of Abraham found themselves in bondage in Egypt, destined to live as slaves with no freedom or hope for themselves, God heard the cries of his people and raised up for them the leader Moses. Throughout the story of humankind is woven the story of God's gracious action on behalf of people everywhere.

Jesus also describes for us various ways to understand how God comes to our aid in the situations that almost overcome us. In the Gospel of Luke Jesus shares a story that illustrates the heart of God for his children:

Is there anyone among you who, if your child asks for a fish, will give a snake instead of a fish? Or if the child asks for an egg, will give a scorpion? If you then, who are evil, know how to give good gifts to your children, how much more will the heavenly Father give the Holy Spirit to those who ask him.

(Luke 11:11-13)

Throughout his ministry, Jesus described God as a loving parent who draws his children close to him. Particularly close to Jesus' heart and concern were the outcast and abandoned. He was there for the sick, the demon-possessed, sinners, children, women, and others who were pushed to the margins of society. The initial experience of Jesus for most people is the experience of Jesus as Savior. That is, they meet him when they are in need and he graciously responds. God is the Savior of those who have a need—and that is all of us.

God is not some impersonal force quite separate and distant from you. God is not a wish concocted by a human brain to fill in the gaps of human ignorance. The experience of the people of God is that God is personal and interacts to save and give life to us. This is the God to whom we pray—a Savior, a Shepherd, a loving Parent, a Healer, a caring One. This God is known through the person of Jesus of Nazareth. And God through Jesus calls us to draw near and ask. Jesus' most direct words about prayer are:

Ask, and it will be given you; search, and you will find; knock, and the door will be opened for you. For everyone who asks receives, and everyone who searches finds, and for everyone who knocks, the door will be opened.

(Luke 11:9-10)

With these words Jesus clearly invites us to allow God to be a part of whatever we need. Countless stories from the Bible and other human experiences demonstrate the saving action of God in response to prayer. God is waiting for the knock on the door. Whoever knocks will find God eager to open it.

Prayer and God's Providence

Why pray if God already knows what is going to happen? Doesn't God predetermine what will take place? This difficult question is not easily solved in a logical way. It is another of those areas of our relationship with God where we are thrown into a paradox. On the one hand, it is true that God is all-knowing and God's purpose will be done. On the other hand, we are commanded and encouraged to pray with all confidence that our prayers make a difference.

When we face such a paradox it is best to act with what we know, rather than with what we do not know. In fact, it is better to act than to become paralyzed. You could spend a lifetime puzzling over this dilemma, trying to arrive at a logical, rational solution and never entering into the act of prayer itself. Or you could let yourself become a total cynic and say that prayer is not real because you cannot understand it or prove it by some scientific method.

Historically, some philosophers and even some cultures have thought of the future as totally fixed. They have tried to express this by devising a philosophy of fate: what will be, will be. In the biblical tradition, however, we find a call to change. God withholds judgment when sinners repent. People are healed when their life is offered to God. People change their minds when confronted by God's truth. The act of prayer is found in all of these situations.

In the Book of Genesis you can read the story of Abraham pleading for the cities of Sodom and Gomorrah. Each time he prays, God consents to withhold judgment if enough righteous people are found. In the end there are not enough and the cities are destroyed, but God was willing to change the judgment (Genesis 18:20-33).

In the New Testament, Jesus teaches about persistence in prayer. In Luke's Gospel we read this parable and teaching:

Then Jesus told them a parable about their need to pray always and not to lose heart. He said, "In a certain city there was a judge who neither feared God nor had respect for people. In that city there was a widow who kept coming to him and saying, 'Grant me justice against my opponent.' For a while he refused; but later he said to himself, 'Though I have no fear of God and no respect for anyone, yet because this widow keeps bothering me, I will grant her justice, so that she may not wear me out by continually coming.'" And the Lord said, "Listen to what the unjust judge says. And will not God grant justice to his chosen ones who cry to him day and night? Will he delay long in helping them? I tell you, he will quickly grant justice to them. And yet, when the Son of Man comes, will he find faith on earth".   *(Luke 18:1-8)*

The closing question in that text has a haunting feel about it. Will God's people pray with such persistence, confident that their prayer will change things? Will faith cut through the paradox between an all-knowing God and the possibility that prayer changes things?

In his explanation of the Lord's Prayer, Martin Luther adds to this discussion when he writes about the phrase "Your will be done, on earth as in heaven." Luther's explanation says, "The good and gracious will of God is surely done without our prayer, but we ask in this prayer that it may be done also among us."[1] Typical of Luther, he does not dismiss either part of the paradox. On the one hand the will of God will be done, but on the other hand he affirms the role of prayer in seeking that God's will be done in particular situations.

Prayer changes things. Trust in the examples of faith and in your own call to prayer to enter into this exciting dialog with God.

Intercessory Prayer

Beyond praying for your own needs, you are encouraged to pray for others. This ministry of prayer is a part of your call to serve others. It is part of what is called the priesthood of all believers. As a Christian you are to be an active participant in the redeeming, caring, and consoling work of God.

Intercession is the prayer you engage in for the sake of others. Throughout the New Testament, we read of requests for intercessory prayer. Paul often requests such prayers, and also includes them in the letters he writes:

> *For this reason, since the day we heard it, we have not ceased praying for you and asking that you may be filled with the knowledge of God's will in all spiritual wisdom and understanding.* (Colossians 1:9)

Prayer is a bond between all Christians. It is a way of affirming the body of Christ. Prayer is a spiritual link in the connections we have with one another and in our ministry with each other. It helps strengthen the Christian community in its struggle against the forces of sin and evil. The Letter to the Ephesians urges us to fulfill this type of prayer ministry for the church today, just as Paul urged it in his time:

> *Pray in the Spirit at all times in every prayer and supplication. To that end keep alert and always persevere in supplication for all the saints. Pray also for me, so that when I speak, a message may be given to me to make known with boldness the mystery of the gospel, for which I am an ambassador in chains. Pray that I may declare it boldly, as I must speak.* (Ephesians 6:18-20)

There is no more important ministry in the church than the ministry of intercessory prayer. A multitude of people need your prayer. Remember your pastor, other leaders in the church, and all those who share in your life in the congregation. The strength of the fellowship and ministry in any congregation is heavily dependent upon this ministry of prayer on behalf of one another.

Intercessory prayer can play another role in your Christian life. It can provide you with many opportunities for ministry. If you assume a ministry of intercession for someone, you might begin to experience a desire to become an active part of the answer to that prayer. If the situation is one where you can make a difference, your loving words might soon become loving action. Intercessory prayer might hold yet another surprise for you, particularly if you are praying for change in another person with whom you are involved.

Intercessory prayer might bring change in you before it affects the one for whom you are praying. Often the key to effective intercessory prayer for another is your openness to change within yourself. You might need to purify your motives and see the other with new eyes. In fact, love must be the motive for intercessory prayer—love that God places in your heart.

Intercession for others allows you to be a channel of God's caring love. If you feel drawn to people's needs and have a strong sense of God's compassion in you, then this type of prayer would be important for you to explore more deeply. *(Praying for Friends and Enemies: Intercessory Prayer* [Minneapolis: Augsburg Fortress, 1995] would be helpful in this exploration.)

Prayer and Healing

In a survey taken in 1993, people said that they prayed most often about issues related to health. This is not such a surprising fact, since our health, or a lack of it, affects us in so many ways. Ill health can disrupt our emotions, economics, relationships, hopes, and sense of self-worth. When we suffer disease, we realize our vulnerability and mortality and know that our lives are susceptible to dramatic change. Even with all of the advances in health care, our encounter with disease, illness, and sickness is still a major concern—one that has always been addressed by religious people in their prayers.

In Christianity, praying for and experiencing healing has been a part of the tradition of the church. It is rooted in the witness to healing found in the Bible. Early in Israel's history, just after the liberation and exodus from Egypt, God declared to them, "I am the Lord who heals you" (Exodus 15:26). In addition, there are many stories of prayer and healing found in the lives of Moses, Isaiah, Elijah, and others in the Old Testament. Such stories can be found in Numbers 21:4-9; Isaiah 38:1-8; 1 Kings 17:17-24; 2 Kings 5:1-14.

The New Testament records numerous stories of prayer and healing, particularly in the ministry of Jesus. In the Gospels of Matthew, Mark, and Luke, one-third of all the writing is related to the healing ministry of Jesus. The gospel stories about Jesus show a broad healing ministry related to the forgiveness of sins, the curing of lepers, giving sight to the blind, making the lame walk, casting out demons, and raising the dead. Also, when Jesus sent out his disciples on missions to the surrounding area, he told them to preach, teach, and heal. This ministry continued in the early church, as indicated by many stories in the book of Acts (Acts 3:1-10; 9:10-20; 9:46-31; 19:11-12; 20:7-12; 28:7-10). The number of stories indicates that praying for healing was a normal practice in the early church.

Praying for healing has always been a part of the ministry of the church, but it has received varying degrees of attention at different times. Today there seems to be a revived interest in prayer and healing. Denominations are publishing services of healing, and many congregations provide opportunities for healing prayers in their public ministry. However, prayers for healing should not be confined to the worshiping congregation. They can be a part of every Christian's prayer life. (See *Praying for Wholeness and Healing* [Minneapolis: Augsburg Fortress, 1995] for a more complete discussion of healing prayer.)

Prayer as Request

Prayer as request has a particular rhythm. We come to God in humility and honest repentance, accepting God's forgiveness. We come to God in faith, expecting God to answer. We receive God's answer in faith and give thanks for God's care and response.

Some people find it hard to ask for anything. Their pride or individualism might be a barrier that makes it hard for them to reach out. God becomes a last resort for them. Doesn't it make more sense to begin with God as the first resource, rather than waiting to speak to God as the last hope?

Help others, especially children, to think of God first whenever they have needs in their life. This does not mean that we do not need to learn to take responsibility and initiative to solve problems, but we should be aware that God is always there to help us. With a lively spirit of prayer that is conscious of God in all moments of life, each of us can learn to put all things into God's presence so that God's transforming power in Jesus Christ can make all things new.

For REFLECTION *and* DISCUSSION

1. Are there things too small or too large for which you do not pray? What are they? How do you decide what to pray for or not to pray for?

2. Do you sense any barriers within yourself that block praying with confidence and trust? What negative thoughts do you have when you ask God for something? Can you find an answer to those negative thoughts?

3. Do you find yourself being more like a fatalist, thinking things will be as they were meant to be, or more like a person who fervently believes prayer changes things? How would each of these views affect the way you pray?

4. Think of a time when you moved from offering prayers for someone to act-ing on their behalf. What prompted you to go beyond the act of praying to become involved in the answer to that prayer? Read James 2:14-16 and describe how this teaching could affect your intercessory prayer life.

5. What struggles do you face when you pray for healing? List your questions about healing prayer and discuss them with someone.

ACTIVITIES

1. For the next few days, practice spontaneous intercessory prayer as you move through the day. Pray for those around you and for situations you become aware of— the street, in your workplace, at home. Direct to God your prayers for blessing or your requests for strangers, coworkers, family mem-bers, or others you meet. Note any changes within yourself or others after you have done this for a while.

2. Develop the discipline of a prayer list, but avoid putting everything and everybody on the list. Pray for those persons and situations to which you feel called. Keeping a list is a helpful reminder to be regular in praying. Think of yourself as a channel of God's love to those for whom you pray.

3. Form an intercessory prayer group. Meet together each week for one-half hour or pray together over the phone. Agree on the things you will pray about and how you will pray for them. Keep a record of prayer projects in your journal and note changes as they occur. Decide together when you will stop praying for someone.

4. Try taking on a long-term prayer project—perhaps a person, a nation, a problem in your community, or a national issue. Pray each day, asking God to bless, surround with love, and bring a solution. You do not need to attempt to solve the problem with your prayer. Hold it up to God and let God work the solution. Continue to pray as long as you feel led to do so.

1.. *The Small Catechism by Martin Luther in Contemporary English with Lutheran Book of Worship Texts (1979 edition),* copyright © 1960, 1968.

Chapter Six

PRAYER *of the* HEART

art of the journey of faith is a desire to experience God's loving presence. In the prayer of the heart, we seek to be still, silent, and focused on God. God is love; therefore, to be in the presence of God is to be in the presence of love. Our prayer is not motivated by the need to ask for or accomplish something. We seek only to know God's love as present and real.

Prayer of the heart is like bringing a vessel to a fountain. In order to be filled with water, the vessel must first be emptied. So, too, you must be separated from your attachments to things, ideas, fantasies, feelings, and concerns. After emptying yourself of attachments, seek a quiet, still place within and wait for a sense of God's presence to fill that emptied space. The prayer of the heart is more like *being* prayer than *doing* prayer.

Throughout the history of the Christian church, certain people have felt called to live a separated, contemplative life. They have pursued God's presence in silence and solitude. This long line of "mystics" stretches from the early church to the present time. In their prayer life they seek to know God in an inner experience of presence and love. However, this form of prayer is not meant for them alone. Any Christian may pursue this form of prayer.

Prayer of the heart was a part of Jesus' pattern of prayer. He often went off by himself to spend long periods in prayer, separating himself from others and the distractions and demands of the crowd. We read in the Gospel of Luke: "Now during those days he went out to the mountain to pray; and he spent the night in prayer to God" (Luke 6:12).

It might help you to understand this type of prayer if you think about the relationship you have with someone you love very much. If you and your loved one are always in the company of other people, you do not have a chance to enjoy being together in an intimate way, focused on each other. Your attention will be drawn to the others around you. If this were to happen most of the time, you would not be able to develop a very deep relationship. Just so, if you desire an intimate relationship with God, set apart times for quietness with God.

Jesus encouraged his disciples to set aside time for this type of prayer as well. In Mark's Gospel Jesus invites his disciples to come away with him and rest in a deserted place (Mark 6:31). Like Jesus himself, they are invited to come away from distraction and focus on God.

The word *rest* in the Bible has a special meaning; it means to be in the presence of God without distraction. Among the Jewish people the Sabbath rest was the setting aside of one day in the week to pay attention to God. The writer of the Letter to the Hebrews speaks of entering God's rest as being in God's eternal presence (Hebrews 4:10-11).

Several Old Testament examples point to this aspect of prayer as important to our relationship with God. We read, "Be still, and know that I am God" (Psalm 46:10). Psalm 42 is often prayed by those who feel a great desire to know God intimately within: "As a deer longs for flowing streams, so my soul longs for you, O God" (Psalm 42:1).

The prophet Elijah had run away in despair, thinking that he alone remained faithful in Israel. He was hiding in a cave in the mountains. The Lord came to him and said that he was about to pass by. Elijah went outside:

> *Now there was a great wind, so strong that it was splitting mountains and breaking rocks in pieces before the Lord, but the Lord was not in the wind; and after the wind an earthquake, but the Lord was not in the earthquake; and after the earthquake a fire, but the Lord was not in the fire; and after the fire a sound of sheer silence. When Elijah heard it, he wrapped his face in his mantle and went out and stood at the entrance of the cave. Then there came a voice to him that said, "What are you doing here, Elijah?"*   *(1 Kings 19:11-13)*

The writings of past mystics show evidence of the way prayer of the heart—this inner journey to know God's presence within—strengthens and provides growth for the spiritual journey. Their descriptions of this type of prayer contain clues for pursuing a deepening prayer journey for yourself.

Today there seems to be a stirring in the souls of many seekers who want a deeper intimacy with God. This stirring has caused many to seek such a prayer experience in Eastern religions, New Age experiments, and revived ancient religious practices. Because they have not heard or seen this practiced in the church, many assume that this form of prayer is not a part of the Christian tradition. However, this tradition does exist within the Christian church and can help us practice this form of prayer in ways that are consistent with the Christian understanding of God and the way God relates to us through Jesus Christ and the Holy Spirit.

Silence, stillness, and solitude. These three words describe the process of moving inward. Silence involves eliminating distractions from the outer world. Stillness refers to the inner calm and avoidance of distractions from within. Solitude is coming to ourselves without distraction so that we can hear the still, small voice of God and experience the loving presence of God—important because of what we face within ourselves and in the world around us.

It should be no secret to any of us that our lives are filled with ourselves. Our desires, needs, thoughts, feelings, and experiences take up most of the room in our awareness and most of our time each day. This is particularly true if our lives are filled with great desires that have a compulsive hold on us. In the prayer of the heart we attempt to empty ourselves of the many distractions that tend to focus our attention on these compulsive thoughts. Many of these addictive patterns are focused on negative responses in our lives: fear, anxiety, anger, or pride. These are disruptive and debilitating, consume vast amounts of energy, and divert us from focusing on God.

Another negative response to life is to take illusions into our lives. In order to defend ourselves or give meaning to life, we often grasp at what is false. Often we are unaware of these illusions, or we assume that they are the way we need to live in order to protect ourselves and make the good life happen. However, this is not the case. Many people have discovered that they had been following a false path. The great theologian Augustine spent the early years of his life pursuing pleasure. When Augustine was finally converted to Christianity, his path took a new direction. He began to live out of God's direction for his life and not out of the compulsive desires of the flesh.

The basic task for all of us, then, is to face up to the question, "Am I walking a road built on an illusion, or am I clearly seeing who I truly am and what God has created me to be?" Thus the prayer of the heart serves an important purpose on our Christian journey. It is part of the process of self-emptying and disillusioning that brings our life into line with the purposes of God.

If we are so focused on ourselves, how does God get in? Various forms of prayer accomplish this purpose. The following descriptions of prayer for the inner journey will provide you with an overview of Christian practices.

One tradition in contemplative prayer focuses on what is called the *apophatic* form of prayer. The emphasis is on the unknowable nature of God. God is so different from us that we cannot with the mind know God as God exists in divine nature. We must leave behind all metaphors, images, and words to seek an inner space devoid of everything so that we might encounter God, who cannot be known through any created means but only in naked love.

Another tradition of contemplative prayer is called the *kataphatic*. Here the emphasis is on meeting the God in whose image we have been created. The journey inward moves with images, metaphors, and words that grow out of the revelation of God in creation and Scripture. This tradition seeks to meet God as God can be known and experienced through God's gracious presence and love. Most Christians probably practice the kataphatic form of contemplative prayer.

More information on the apophatic tradition can be found in *The Cloud of Unknowing*, which is listed in the book list on page 79. The kataphatic tradition can be explored in the writings of Teresa of Avila and Ignatius of Loyola, among others.

In silence, stillness, and solitude, God will be perceived and God's truth will be expressed. You might begin to see yourself more clearly—your weaknesses, strengths, illusions, and commitments. You will come to see Christ more clearly—the beauty, joy, and love he brings you. You will see God's truth more clearly—God's will and purpose for your life.

Contemplative prayer has been criticized by some as an escape from what they would call the real, outer world. However, this view is not borne out by the lives of those who seriously practice contemplative prayer. Teresa of Avila ran several convents and reorganized her whole order while being a contemplative. Thomas Merton, a Trappist monk, was sensitive to the political and social concerns of our day as well as the author of many volumes. Martin Luther, a man of deep prayer, said that the busier he got the more time he had to take for prayer. The busiest homemaker, executive, farmer, pastor, student, or salesperson can practice contemplative prayer.

If you think contemplative prayer means abandoning the world, as critics have said, that is not so. Contemplative prayer actually is a means by which you can become motivated toward action, empowered by love, and kept humble. If you encounter God's love in contemplative prayer, that love will, in turn, move your life toward your neighbor.

The inner journey of prayer has always been a part of the prayer experience of God's people. If your religious experience is limited to external rites or only to what is rational and material, you will miss a large portion of being in Christ and experiencing God's love. In Ephesians the image of this heart knowledge is made clear:

I pray that the God of our Lord Jesus Christ, the Father of glory, may give you a spirit of wisdom and revelation as you come to know him, so that, with the eyes of your heart enlightened, you may know what is the hope to which he has called you, what are the riches of his glorious inheritance among the saints, and what is the immeasurable greatness of his power for us who believe, according to the working of his great power.   *(Ephesians 1:17–19)*

With the image of "the eyes of the heart," the writer points to a real inner experience. It is this experience that the prayer of the heart seeks to find.

Not everyone finds contemplative prayer easy. Some temperaments find it difficult to relate to silence and inwardness. However, there is value for everyone in this type of prayer. Don't think you have to do it just like someone else. Experiment, but be aware of the following points:

- Don't assume every voice you hear within comes from God.
- If you have an experience of God's nearness and love, cherish and learn from it. It might be wise not to share it immediately with others.
- Expect to become aware of things about yourself that should change.
- Remember that change will come slowly.
- Stay close to Christ in your reflection and prayer.
- Test all your experiences against the Bible.
- Pray for humility.

Exploring how others have prayed and reading about the benefits it has brought to their lives is worthwhile. But sooner or later you need to try it on your own. A helpful way to grow in the use of contemplative prayer is to set aside specific periods of time. Commit these times to silence and find a place where you will not be easily disturbed. You can set aside a time each day. Make your prayer period long enough so that your prayer is not rushed. It is better not to have to force yourself into solitude in a hurried manner. Do not think of the time in silence according to clock time. Judge the time spent in solitude according to its quality and purpose. Some days this might be fifteen minutes. Other days it might be an hour. Let go of the time and space factors in controlling contemplative prayer. This is part of what you want to let go in the prayer of the heart. Place yourself before God and wait patiently for God to fill the moments with love and presence.

Some people adopt the discipline of a longer silent prayer period one day a week. It is like a Sabbath rest. The time is filled with contemplative prayer, journaling, scripture reflection, and expressing prayer through drawing, clay, or dance. This becomes a rich time, renewing the relationship you have with your Lord.

I remember a woman whose whole prayer life, and subsequently her life, changed when she attended a three-day silent retreat. She discovered the transforming power of silence and contemplative prayer. As she wrote in her journal about her experiences, she realized in a fresh way how God is willing and able to speak to us within and bring insight and wisdom for self-understanding.

Many different retreat or prayer centers will provide space and hospitality for silent retreats. They might last for a few hours or a few days. Many contemplative pray-ers follow a pattern of annual three-day silent retreats. If you feel uncomfortable or fearful exploring the prayer of the heart on your own, seek out a spiritual director or use a program of guided retreats at a prayer center.

For REFLECTION *and* DISCUSSION

1. Reflect on your most intimate experiences of God's presence. What did you experience? What were the circumstances surrounding the experience? How would you describe the experience of God's love?

2. What barriers do you encounter when you seek to be silent and still in contemplation? Are they primarily physical, mental, or emotional? What, for you, are the fearful aspects of seeking solitude with God? What are the exciting aspects?

3. Have you experienced the difference between entering into contemplative prayer and lying in a hammock, daydreaming? Describe the differences.

4. Contemplative prayer eventually leads one to face false illusions about oneself and offers the opportunity for change. Are you feeling a need for change within yourself? Do you feel an urge to seek God more deeply? Make a list of those things you would most desire to change in your inner life.

ACTIVITIES

1. If you have not done so before, begin to practice a daily quiet time—the discipline of silence and solitude with God. Begin with ten minutes each day. Find a comfortable, quiet place to sit. Make your body comfortable. It is best to sit with your feet on the floor and your arms hanging loosely with your hands resting on your lap. Do not fold your hands. Maintain a posture that will be comfortable for the entire period. It might be helpful to close

your eyes to remove visual distractions. When you begin, pray for the Holy Spirit to be present with you and to protect you in this time when you will be spiritually vulnerable. Following the prayer, take a deep breath and let the tension flow from your body. Let go of the burdens, the tasks before you, and the concerns of the day. Next, focus on your breath. Become conscious of your breath moving in and out. Notice the rhythm of your breathing. Don't force your breathing. Your breathing will become your focus point to return to whenever you are distracted. Soon you will be conscious of the many thoughts racing through your mind. Don't resist them. Acknowledge that they are there and then let them pass by like floating clouds. Return to a focus on your breathing. If your body distracts you, treat it the same as the thoughts. Try not to build any expectations of what you will experience. Allow yourself to remain in the stillness and solitude for as long as it is comfortable. When you end your silent time offer a prayer of thanksgiving. After a few days you will probably find yourself able to extend the time of your silence. Remember, the purpose of your silent time is to experience the presence of God's love. You are seeking God alone. Everything else is a distraction. Treat it as such. This basic approach to silence is a practice that will be used for many other types of contemplative and meditative prayer. It does not come easily. It will take time to develop.

2. A prayer form that developed out of the search to discover what it means to "pray without ceasing" is called the Jesus prayer. This prayer focuses on breathing while repeating the phrase, "Lord Jesus Christ, Son of God, have mercy on me, a sinner." Some people use a shorter phrase like, "Lord Jesus, have mercy" or just the name "Jesus." Begin as you do with contemplative preparation: pray, relax, make your body comfortable, focus on your breathing. The words of the phrase will follow your breathing. As you breath in, say, "Lord Jesus Christ, Son of God." As you breath out, say, "Have mercy on me a sinner." You can say the words out loud or think them in your head, but repeat them over and over again. This prayer will offer a great sense of peace and a sense of God's presence. If you practice it frequently, it will become an ongoing prayer, linked to each breath. Some people speak of waking up in the morning with this prayer going on within them.

3. To help develop the spirit of contemplative prayer, read one of the books listed in "For Further Reading." It would be helpful to discuss your reading and your experience with others.

Chapter Seven

PRAYER *as* ENLIGHTENMENT

o pray is to have your mind, heart, and senses opened to God and to life around you. Prayer is not an escape from facing who you are or what you are called to be and to do. Prayer is part of that process of becoming—the unfolding of your life in a world God has created and the directing of your life with the purpose God has in mind.

Prayer is not a substitute for struggling and learning to unravel the mystery of who you are or what your life purpose is. Through prayer we enter into the struggle. It is one of the tools a Christian can use in the search for enlightenment and the process of discernment. Prayer is a particular way of listening to God, the Scriptures, your Christian community, and the whole human community around you.

A form of prayer that focuses on a particular issue or question in order to gain wisdom is called meditation. If contemplation is seeking to experience the heart of God, meditation is seeking to know the mind of God. When you pray with your focus on a particular issue, you try to hear what God has to say. It might have to do with understanding yourself, finding a direction, or discerning God's will. Your reflection could focus on understanding a passage of Scripture, choices that you have to make, your next steps in spiritual growth, or obstacles that you want to remove from your path.

Meditation and contemplation make use of similar methods. When meditating, begin by seeking silence and removing all distractions. Look for a place within from which God may speak to the issues confronting you. Then you might ponder the Bible, spiritual advice from others, readings, or simply wait for an inner illumination. Whatever the focus of your meditation, the point is to seek wisdom—a sense of how to apply knowledge in a practical and direct way.

Seeking God's Wisdom

Linking God's word with meditation is an important part of the Christian's journey to wisdom. Wisdom from God enables us to live in accordance with God's will. The Bible encourages us to pray for wisdom:

> *If any of you is lacking in wisdom, ask God, who gives to all generously and ungrudgingly, and it will be given you. But ask in faith, never doubting, for the one who doubts is like a wave of the sea, driven and tossed by the wind.*
>
> *(James 1:5-6)*

Another way to describe wisdom is to say that although this special knowledge might begin in your head, ultimately it is about your heart. For example, if you study the Scriptures only to understand them objectively, you can lose the personal nature of Christ in the word. Rather than looking at the Scriptures as something to be taken into a laboratory to be put under a microscope, think of the Scriptures as the microscope examining you. Or, as the Letter of James suggests, think of the word as a mirror in which you are revealed to yourself. James's caution is, don't see the image and walk away forgetting what you saw. Rather, see the image of yourself and then go and do what it directs. Understanding the Bible intellectually is important, but ultimately the Word is meant to affect your whole life by its presence within you. That is wisdom.

The wisdom sought in meditation might also be described as enlightenment or illumination. The inner reflection that takes place in meditation is a bridge between a question, decision, or concern in your life and God's direction about that concern. You want to perceive God's word as it applies to your life. Like a midwife, the Holy Spirit uses meditative prayer to bring to birth in you the life and light that is Jesus. The Spirit nurtures meditation by the Word of God. That Word is present in the Bible, in the Sacraments, in the fellowship of Christians, and in prayerful silence within. These are the same Word: Jesus Christ.

Meditation on Scripture

Dietrich Bonhoeffer, a theologian who lived in Germany during the 1930s, wrote a book on Christian community and devoted much of it to reflection on prayer and the presence of God's Word in the community of faith. He wrote in his book *Life Together*:

> *We are silent at the beginning of the day because God should have the first word, and we are silent before going to sleep because the last word also belongs to God. We keep silence solely for the sake of the Word. This stillness before the Word will exert its influence upon the whole day.* [1]

You might take with you into your time of silence a portion of Scripture and reflect on how it relates to your life. One way to reflect upon Scripture or other material is to approach it prayerfully. Begin with prayer, seeking to put yourself in a receptive mode. Slowly read the text, perhaps more than once. Think about its meaning and notice any particular phrases or images from the text that catch your attention. Center yourself in quietness and stillness and keep the Word before your mind. Be together with the Word, focused and attentive to it. Examine it from many sides. Write down insights and understandings that come to you. Close your meditation with a prayer of thanksgiving.

Ignatius Loyola taught a method of Scripture reflection that uses the senses and imagination in the meditative process. This works particularly well for stories from the Gospels or Old Testament. Read the passage, noticing all the persons involved, where it took place, and any other descriptive words in the story. Take the scene with you into silence and let the scene play out in your imagination. See the people. Feel the breeze. Smell the flowers. Notice people's reactions. Let the scene be rebuilt within you and speak to you as you find yourself in the middle of the story.

Since Jesus Christ is the way—the path you seek to follow—enlightenment will come as you meditate on God's word, and especially on Jesus' life and teaching. You focus on Jesus in order to think and respond biblically with your life. You are seeking the mind of Christ within yourself. In his Letter to the Colossians, the apostle Paul writes about what could be understood as the goal of Christian enlightenment—the path illuminated by the presence of God's Word within you:

> *Let the word of Christ dwell in you richly; teach and admonish one another in all wisdom; and with gratitude in your hearts sing psalms, hymns, and spiritual songs to God. And whatever you do, in word or deed, do everything in the name of the Lord Jesus, giving thanks to God the Father through him .*
> *(Colossians 3:16-17)*

Discernment

Another important aspect of meditative prayer is discernment—the process of discovering God's will in a particular situation and being persuaded to follow it. In addition to listing the positive and negative results of a certain action, you can also take your question to God in reflective prayer. Enter your silent time and bring your question with you. Wait for God to speak to you about it. Your question might be answered quite directly through a sense of peace that comes with a certain decision. Or you might eliminate certain answers based on the negative response you feel. As you meditate in a discerning process, expect that God might first help you clarify or challenge your motives. Be prepared to be changed. Be prepared, also, to wait. Often the discernment process will take time.

At times, the discernment process can include praying with others about the decision. You might bring the advice or counsel of friends into your quiet time to discern its truth for you. Or you can enlist friends to pray with you in a meditative way. This can provide both support and confirmation of a decision. Jesus indicated that praying with others would enhance this discerning process.

Again, truly I tell you, if two of you agree on earth about anything you ask, it will be done for you by my Father in heaven. For where two or three are gathered in my name, I am there among them .   *(Matthew 18:19-20)*

Including others in the discerning process allows them to confirm or deny your own leanings. The important element here is not that the number of people increases the effectiveness of prayer, but that a consensus among believers can confirm that an action is God's will.

Jesus' meditation in the Garden of Gethsemane before his crucifixion illuminates another aspect of prayer and the discerning process. Jesus knew God's will for him. As he faced the cross he sought to discern whether this was the only way. The prospect of the bearing the weight of the world's sin and confronting death threw Jesus into an agony. Jesus sought confidence that this was truly God's path for him and asked for strength to walk in that path.

You might come to know God's will in prayer but then face obstacles in carrying out that will. Fear, anxiety, pride, or loss of possessions might paralyze you. You might have to spend time deep in prayer with God, seeking God's help to overcome these obstacles before you can act on what you have discovered as God's will for you.

Focusing on the Positive

The things you allow your mind to dwell on shape much of life. You might, from time to time, find yourself struggling with a particular issue. Your active, petitioning prayer might be that God will change you, but your meditation or reflection time might be focused on the very thing you want removed. Moral struggles against lust, gambling, laziness, or envy might be lost because they are the object of all of your thoughts, fantasies, or inward reflection. Too many Christians focus their verbal prayers—which take a few moments—on moral goodness, but spend hours of inward reflection on negative thoughts.

In Philippians, the apostle Paul gives wise counsel about focusing your thoughts on things that will edify your life:

> *Finally, beloved, whatever is true, whatever is honorable, whatever is just, whatever is pure, whatever is pleasing, whatever is commendable, if there is any excellence and if there is anything worthy of praise, think about these things.*
> *(Philippians 4:8)*

A Word of Caution

One caution about meditative practices: be careful to distinguish between fantasy and prayer images, between daydreaming and prayerful meditation. Fantasy is an inward flight of wish fulfillment, desire, or escape from a harsh reality. Usually, it is not rooted in a promise of God or based on the reality of your life. Often it is an expression of a desire rooted in the flesh, rather than the spirit. It tends to be self-centered and ego gratifying. Not all fantasy is bad; however, it should not be confused with prayer.

Meditative prayer uses the imagination as a God-given part of who you are. In prayer the imagination is inspired by the Spirit to give form to the prayer. Imagination allows the pray-er to visualize the subject of the meditation. Imagination, then, becomes an instrument of the Spirit to edify you and give you knowledge. Meditative prayer is a part of your journey to holiness and sanctification and not a part of fantasies that will destroy your moral character and behavior.

As you move forward in your prayer journey, meditation will be an important part of your growth. It will provide a positive means of enlightenment by the word of God for your life. Your discernment of God's will for yourself will be strengthened, and you will be edified for a life that reflects holiness and wholesomeness.

For REFLECTION *and* DISCUSSION

1. Wisdom is the ability to apply knowledge in the most direct, helpful, and specific way. In what important ways has the wisdom in the Bible affected your life? What was the wisdom you encountered? How was your life changed because of it?

2. How have Scripture and prayer been related in your devotional life? What possibilities do you now see to link them more closely together?

3. The chapter presents several ways you can make use of prayer of enlightenment: to grow in self-knowledge, to discern God's will, and to seek direction and strength relating to moral issues. In what ways have you used meditation for any of these areas of your life? What was the result? If you have not prayed in this fashion, how do you react to using prayer in this way?

ACTIVITIES

1. Choose one of the following Bible passages for a meditation exercise: Luke 5:1-11; Luke 10:38-42; Luke 12:22-34; Luke 18:35-43. Try meditating in the following pattern:
    A. Quiet yourself in a relaxed position. Shrug off the burdens and cares of the day.
    B. Pray for the Holy Spirit's presence and guidance in this meditative time.
    C. Without pausing, read the scripture text you have chosen.
    D. Slowly reread the text. Pause at the end of each sentence and recall what you have just read.
    E. Notice any words or images that caught your attention and focus on them. What questions arise in your mind? How is this sentence related to your life? Remain silent with this text. Follow each avenue of thought about this text as it comes to mind.
    F. At the close of your reflection time, offer a prayer of thanksgiving.
    G. In your journal, write any insights or questions that are important to you.

2. Some find it helpful to use their imaginations in Scripture meditation. Choose one of the Bible passages from the first activity or choose another

passage for this exercise. As you read the text, notice carefully all the references that provide background information about the story: time of day, mood, environment, weather, the particular people involved, Jesus' attitude and behavior, people's reactions to Jesus. Move slowly through the story, using your imagination to visualize the complete scene. Identify as much as possible with the scene and the people involved. This will help you discover the human experience of those who encountered Jesus and enhance your own encounter with him through this text.

3. Think of a decision you have to make. Prepare to meditate on this decision. Bring your questions and choices into your solitude and seek insight from God as you reflect on the situation. If you have a prayer partner or spiritual friend, invite that person to meditate on the issue for discernment and to share thoughts with you. This process can help to either confirm or question your own insights.

4. Occasionally, to enhance your spiritual understanding or growth, you might want to meditate on an object: the cross, an icon, a picture, a symbol (such as the rainbow—God's promise to Noah, the dove—God's Holy Spirit, or a candle—Christ as the light of the world).

1. Dietrich Bonhoeffer, *Life Together* (New York: Harper and Row), p. 79.

Chapter Eight

PRAYER *as* COMPLAINT

rayer has political and social dimensions. In the give-and-take of society and people's daily comings and goings, suffering and injustice become very evident. There are victims and victimizers. People win and people lose. Some control and others are controlled. Power is misused. Violence breaks lives apart. People are rejected and marginalized.

An ancient prayer of the church has been spoken by people of every generation who have been downtroddened, overcome, forced to suffer unjustly, and abandoned. People have prayed, "*Kyrie eleison.* Lord, have mercy!" With this prayer, people have cried out their pain and anguish to God. It has been spoken by those in need and by those who want to identify with the suffering ones. "Lord, have mercy" is the prayer that tells God the situation is too big for you to handle. It is the honest expression of complaint to God that things are not right and are too overwhelming for you to change.

It is important to pray congruently with your feelings and the human situation. That is, your words should honestly and accurately reflect your experience. Too often Christians have been unwilling to share with God their pain, sorrow, or anger. They have been afraid that others would judge them as "not Christian enough" if they admitted they were suffering. This notion is based on the assumption that faithful Christians never suffer and should always be smiling. It is true that Christians receive strong support from God and the knowledge that God always cares for us. Yet the cries of God's people in the Bible are unmistakable. They honestly offer up their pain, their sorrow, and their anger at injustice.

You are not less a Christian if you experience sorrow, pain, anguish, or righteous indignation. God heard the cries of his people suffering in Egypt.

Jesus heard the cry for mercy from blind Bartimaeus. And God hears and honors our prayers of complaint and the cries of our hearts. Perhaps one of the reasons people sometimes do not experience salvation or healing is that they will not admit they are suffering pain, sorrow, or righteous indignation. A healthy sob or wail is often the beginning of healing and transformation.

I was teaching at a weekend retreat. In the opening sentence of a worship service, I referred to being abandoned. The word had barely left my mouth when a woman in the front row began to sob and then to wail. When I spoke with her after the service, I discovered that her deepest pain had to do with a sense of abandonment, but that she never allowed herself to think that word or express her pain. At the moment I used the word, her pain would be held no longer. It burst from her—a true heart-cry. That prayer of pain, bursting forth like a broken boil, began a healing process.

Loneliness is a mark of our time. Many lack intimacy with others and with God but they try to cover their loneliness with a veneer of lightheartedness and manufactured joy. God's invitation to pray is an invitation to intimacy. God seeks to reach across the abyss to unite with us in an experience of deep fellowship and belonging. If you resist or suppress the pain, anger, or loneliness you feel, you cannot respond to invitations to intimacy. The cry-of-the-heart prayer means giving yourself over to God's justice and mercy. It is part of the process of dealing with loss, despair, or hurt. It gives voice to your experience. It is the cry of reality.

The Cry of Righteous Anger

Injustice provokes anger. When you are aware that you or someone else is being treated unjustly or being victimized, your hurt and frustration can turn to anger. Rather than repressing these feelings or allowing them to turn into vengeful violence, you can express the frustration and anger in prayer. When Jesus spoke about loving our enemies and praying for them, he offered us another way to respond to injustice. Rather than letting anger become violence directed by self-pity or revenge, he showed us how to undergird with prayer whatever prophetic word or action we might take. And prayer that is rooted in love for our enemy leads to action in accord with God's heart for justice and freedom. Our prayer and actions are no longer just personal, ego-driven campaigns to get even or hurt someone.

A Christian gives voice to personal feelings but then seeks to channel prayer and response according to God's justice in a spirit of love and transformation. For example, Jesus expressed his frustration with people who refused to see in him God's gift of life and hope. Jesus' lament reads: "How often have I desired to gather your children together as a hen gathers her brood under her wings, and you were not willing!" (Matthew 23:37b).

Jesus also sought to respond lovingly to his enemies. Jesus did not set out on a personal vendetta to destroy his enemies, so when he was arrested in the Garden of Gethsemane he told his disciples to put away their swords. The issue was much larger than Jesus' personal safety or vindication.

Much of today's violence on the streets demonstrates anger and frustration at work. The violence does not create a new society or bring resolution to social problems. But we can all learn from Jesus' response to anger, and in our own time we also have models like Gandhi and Martin Luther King Jr., people who rooted their prophetic response to injustice in a deep spirituality that connected them to God's vindication of his people. By acting and teaching as they did, Jesus, Gandhi, and King tried to follow God's lead and keep their struggles from becoming mere platforms for personal vengeance or irresponsible violence.

Consider this homely illustration of one person's failure to respond appropriately to his pain. A man is rudely awakened by some disparaging words from his wife. He buries his response within, but all day long he spreads his anger out by his rude treatment of the bus driver, coworkers, and the family dog. By repressing his frustration and anger he does not solve the problem. Instead he takes his anger out on others. In the end, he finds no true satisfaction or resolution.

How do we deal with our righteous anger? Prayer is part of the process of moving from awareness to action in matters of injustice. There are three distinct ways of praying. First, give voice to the cry in your heart. As with feelings of pain, anguish, or loneliness, express your feelings honestly and often. Continue this until you are ready to move on. Second, prayerfully allow God to help you to love your enemies. This, too, might take some time. Finally, follow God's lead in seeking justice and freedom.

The cry of the heart in righteous anger might not always be about ourselves. It might refer to someone else's situation. Compassion for situations of injustice, whether for one person or a group in society, might cause you to want to respond with some kind of action. Again, it is important that you be rooted in prayer so that you are motivated by understanding God's will. Praying about justice, like all prayer, means offering the situation up to God, following God's lead in taking action, and then seeing how God will take care of it. The results of prayer are always in God's hands, God's time, and through God's means.

When you are moved by compassion to cry out in righteous anger, often the next step is to get personally involved. Prayer is not a substitute for what God might want to do through you to answer the prayer and transform the situation. Very often, though, prayer becomes a prelude to action. The questions that follow the heart-cry for justice might be, "What can I do about it?" "How can I make a difference?" "Where do I go from here?" "Am I contributing to the problem?" These questions might lead you to continue your prayer in another form: action on behalf of the oppressed.

The Cry for Mercy

Many situations in life require that you ask for help from beyond your own resources or strength. You might, however, not be willing to ask for such help. Sometimes you might feel that you deserve what is happening to you. Many people think they have no right to ask for mercy and expect to have to pay for their sins. They may have been shamed to the point where they dare not ask for help. At other times they might feel threatened by any show of weakness or vulnerability and will try to go it alone. Such stoicism can rob a person of the help they really need. The gospel stories about Jesus encourage us to believe in the mercy God offers. God invites us to come out from behind shame, guilt, and pride to stand in the light of God's mercy.

Can you imagine the wonderful surprise when a homeless, rejected, dying person on the streets of Calcutta is tenderly picked up and carried to a clean bed and surrounded by loving, touching people? Mother Teresa and her workers embody for hundreds what it means to have the cry for mercy heard. She lives out what we read in the pages of the New Testament: Jesus' acceptance and mercy offered to those bowed down with shame and guilt. "Lord, have mercy" is the cry on the lips of the blind, the woman pleading for her daughter, and so many others. Encouraged by Jesus' invitation, all who came found themselves accepted and helped, no matter what they had done or who they were.

This type of prayer expresses what is in the heart. It is not meant to be an explanation or rationalization, just a cry for mercy. There is no need to explain or to justify yourself. Trusting in God's mercy, you cry to God from the heart.

Jesus told this parable as an example of the cry of the heart:

> *Two men went up to the temple to pray, one a Pharisee and the other a tax collector. The Pharisee, standing by himself, was praying thus, "God, I thank you that I am not like other people: thieves, rogues, adulterers, or even like this tax collector. I fast twice a week; I give a tenth of all my income." But the tax collector, standing far off, would not even look up to heaven, but was beating his breast and saying, "God, be merciful to me a sinner!" I tell you, this man went down to his home justified rather than the other.* (Luke 18:10-14)

The Pharisee covered over his guilt with rationalization and comparison. He was not able to receive mercy because he felt he had no need for it. The tax collector offered a simple cry from the heart. His cry was what he truly felt, and in no way did he try to dismiss it or mask it. He left the temple with a clean heart. The other, because of his repressed guilt, left with a harder heart, unable to receive or give mercy. He was more apt to judge than to forgive because he refused to acknowledge what was in his heart.

The Cry of Abandonment

The pain of rejection and abandonment is another of the deep heart-cries of many people. Whether the pain comes from a childhood memory or a more recent experience, rejection and abandonment create a deep ache.

As humans we have been made for fellowship and relationship. Loneliness denies a meaningful part of what it is to be a human being. Experiences of abandonment and rejection can create a bitter and cynical spirit if allowed to fester within. Trust becomes difficult for anyone who has been abandoned. But often those who have had such experiences deny or at least do not express them. Such repression stifles a healthy prayer relationship with God because at a deep level we fear that we will be abandoned by God, just as we have been abandoned by others.

In our contemporary society many people have experienced a variety of abusive situations. People respond to these experiences in ways similar to abandonment because the basic issue is the same: trust has been broken and the person has been separated from someone whom he or she loved. Because of the deep trauma involved, a person who has been abused might repress his or her feelings for a long time. When these feelings finally do break out and begin to express themselves, it creates an upheaval in the emotional and spiritual life of the person. Prayer becomes difficult. The person might ask, "Why did God allow this to happen? Why did God abandon me in the situation? Why didn't God protect me?"

Healing is available for the person who has experienced such profound pain. Jesus' heart-cry of abandonment on the cross, "My God, my God, why have you forsaken me," encourages us to speak what is often left unspoken. When you acknowledge and express the pain of rejection or loneliness in your heart, healing can begin. A heart deeply scarred by the wounds of abandonment needs to cry aloud. God hears the heart-cry of abandonment, victimization, and loneliness. As King David declared when he offered up his pain, "A broken and contrite heart, O God, you will not despise" (Psalm 51:17).

For REFLECTION *and* DISCUSSION

1. In what ways do you experience what is called "the absence of God"? How does it affect your prayer life?

2. Do you feel comfortable expressing anger toward God when you experience or witness injustice or overwhelming struggle? Why or why not?

3. Some say that loneliness is the deepest pain of our present culture. In what ways do you experience loneliness? Contemplative prayer is an avenue to help shift loneliness to solitude. Have you experienced the difference between loneliness and solitude? How might a deepened relationship with God minister to your loneliness?

4. Reflect on the difference between judgment and mercy. How does each of them affect the way you might pray for yourself or others? How difficult is it for you to ask for help or mercy? What attitudes block your ability to ask for mercy?

5. How do you respond to the idea that prayer should be congruent with your feelings? Do you agree that giving voice to your feelings is the beginning of a healing process? What feelings do you tend to hide from God?

ACTIVITIES

1. Discuss with others the role of prayer in dealing with anger. What experience have you had resolving anger through prayer?

2. Spend a few days focusing prayers on news items that affect you emotionally, either positively or negatively. Ask God to direct those prayers with the gift of love. Continue praying for those persons or situations as long as you feel led to do so. Notice what changes occur within yourself. Notice any changes taking place in those situations.

3. What issues in your family, community, or nation affect you deeply? Begin to pray for them and for direction in finding ways to become involved in the solution. Discuss with others the relationship between prayer and action.

Chapter Nine

PRAYER *as* JUBILATION

ubilation is a word that sounds like what it means. It explodes out of the mouth with breath and energy. It means the expression of great joy. It can refer either to the act of exalting another, or to the lifting up of your own mind or spirit.

When applied to prayer, jubilation can relate to both meanings. Jubilant prayer does involve the exaltation of God—proclaiming the honor and glory that belongs to God—but it also describes the state of the pray-er when such prayer is offered. When you exalt God, your own spirit is lifted up in joy and gratitude. Jubilation is the interaction between exalting God and experiencing within yourself the uplifting of your spirit. Both of these are important in the experience of prayer. The motive for jubilation is to acknowledge God. One of the effects is to experience joy within yourself.

The Christian's experience of joy is not generated from within or dependent on outer circumstances. The source of joy is God. Knowing God and experiencing God's presence brings joy to life. Joy, it has been said, is a sure sign of God's presence. Joy is listed as one of the effects of the Holy Spirit's presence in the life of the Christian in Galatians: "By contrast, the fruit of the Spirit is love, joy..." (Galatians 5:22).

Our good feelings can come from many sources. Compliments make you feel good. Success makes you feel good. Having your life in balance makes you feel good. But many things in life can also cause you to feel bad. Both good and bad feelings are emotional responses to life situations. Your inner disposition can affect your emotions as well and make you feel up or down. Joy as a fruit of the Spirit, however, is not limited to emotional response or inner disposition.

Rather, it is related to knowledge and faith, as well as to feeling. Knowing who God is and believing in God's steadfast love for you is the foundation of this type of joy. When you immerse yourself in this knowledge and trust, the exaltation of God flows from you and in turn elevates your mind and spirit.

Prayers of jubilation are made up of two types of prayer: praise and thanksgiving. Praise is the prayer that exalts God for being God. Thanksgiving is the prayer that exalts God for what God has done or given.

Prayer as Praise

Praise is a facet of faith. Belief in God as the Creator and Redeemer of your life will bring you to the act of praise and adoration. You are known by God and loved by God. Could there ever be a better reason to exalt and glorify the name of God?

I am often amazed watching people leave a worship service with their eyes downcast, their mouths turned down, and a scowl on their face. God's word has been shared, God's glorious deeds displayed, and love expressed in a personal way, and yet the spirit of praise was not expressed. Joy is not evident in their faces or manner. It might be that praise has not been a part of their prayer experience or that the fruits of praise are not among their expectations. It might be that their inner eyes are focused on those things that have led them to the down side of life. It is possible to become so preoccupied with problems that the glory and wonder of God are not visible.

Praise flows from a vision of the glory and majesty of God. Praise emerges from the experience of God's overwhelming love and grace in Christ Jesus. Praise erupts at the realization of the indwelling Spirit of God. That is the reason that so often in Scripture the admonition to praise is preceded by an accounting of God's creative power and compassionate love:

> *We ponder your steadfast love, O God,*
> *in the midst of your temple.*
> *Your name, O God, like your praise,*
> *reaches to the ends of the earth.*
> *(Psalm 48:9-10)*

Prayers of praise arise from remembering who God is. In the midst of all that is petty, mean, low-spirited, and depressing in the world, the memory of God will lead you to the place of praise. In praising you will be lifted above that environment to taste the joy of the Lord once again. The psalmist David wrote while he hid in the wilderness when he was being hunted down to be killed. You would expect a total lament from him. However, he wrote:

O God, you are my God, I seek you,
      my soul thirsts for you;
my flesh faints for you,
      as in a dry and weary land where there is no water.
So I have looked upon you in the sanctuary,
      beholding your power and glory.
Because your steadfast love is better than life,
      my lips will praise you.
So I will bless you as long as I live;
      I will lift up my hands and call on your name.
My soul is satisfied as with a rich feast,
      and my mouth praises you with joyful lips
when I think of you on my bed,
      and meditate on you in the watches of the night;
for you have been my help,
      and in the shadow of your wings I sing for joy.
                    (Psalm 63:1-7)

This experience is echoed in the New Testament in the journeys of the apostle Paul. In Philippi, he and Barnabas were thrown into prison. In the middle of the night they were up praying and singing hymns. An earthquake freed them from prison.

God is worthy of praise. God never demands praise yet receives it as people realize the personal existence of the Creator and Jesus Christ. Time and time again, Christians have discovered that if they will remember who God is in power and love and if they offer praise and exalt God, a change will occur. Praise will lift their vision and spirits and set them on the high Rock.

It is interesting to note that one of the temptations of Jesus in the wilderness was for him to bow down and adore the devil. The devil was seeking from Jesus what he did not deserve or have title to: adoration and praise. That alone belongs to God. When you consistently and eagerly offer praise in prayer to God, you are not allowing yourself to be tempted to adore something or someone else in God's place. You can make prayers of praise a part of each day's devotion so that God remains the only one worthy to receive your praise.

Praise is also an antidote to pride. It is possible to fall into the habit of viewing God as something of an errand person—someone who waits in the anteroom, ready to be called upon whenever something is needed. You might begin to hold on to the reins of your life and gradually elevate yourself to the top position. Praise will soon become difficult and will be something you avoid if pride gains so much power in your life.

All things are made to praise their Maker, and this praise will be endless. A mark of our commitment to God in Jesus Christ is praise. As creatures of God with all the rest of creation, we are called upon to bear witness to God's worthiness to be praised.

Prayer as Thanksgiving

A companion to the prayer of praise is the prayer of thanksgiving. Like the prayer of praise, thanksgiving begins with an inner awareness and attitude. This awareness is summarized in the Letter of James: "Every generous act of giving, with every perfect gift, is from above, coming down from the Father of lights, with whom there is no variation or shadow due to change" (James 1:17).

Everything you have is a gift from God. Underlying all the ways your life has been blessed with food, clothing, family, friends, nature, work, play, and possessions is the hand of God. All spiritual, material, social, and mental reality has come into being through God's creative power. "In him we live and move and have our being" (Acts 17:28).

The Christian community has always understood and confessed that God is the Creator of all and that all things exist in God. If you consciously live with this awareness, gratitude becomes an automatic response. However, as humans we are not without our struggle at this point. It is difficult to remember and express thanksgiving at all times. More and more of the world around us bears the mark of human creativity rather than God's. We can process food and change the environment. It begins to seem as if all that we have is a product of human ingenuity. This is especially true in urban environments. Animals, forests, plains, and beautiful wild streams are not something we encounter daily. We do not have the daily reminders of the natural process of planting and harvesting. Add to this the natural human tendency to take ownership of what is in reach and you have the makings of a person who might find it difficult to remember that God is behind all that exists.

A deep awareness of God's role in creating and sustaining life often begins through a spiritual awakening as God becomes real in a saving, healing, or redeeming way. As the good news of Jesus Christ takes root in a person's life, he or she begins a journey to learn the meaning of giving thanks. As more and more of life is touched by an awakened faith, God's relationship to all aspects of life gradually become clear. Gratitude to God might be extended to more and more areas of life. Soon, with the growth of the Spirit, the Christian discovers there is nothing that has not been provided by God.

However, that scenario is not as simple as it sounds. Every Christian, no matter how mature, struggles to maintain an attitude of gratitude. A friend of mine who is a mature and aware Christian told me the story about a day he had a rude awakening. He was lying on an air mattress on the lake where he had his cabin. He looked at the tall pines on the shore. The blue sky above had a few puffs of clouds. He noticed a family of ducks swimming by. He began to reminisce about how far he had come from his boyhood poverty. In a moment of exaltation he cried out, "Mine! All mine!" Then, in a moment of repentance he said, "O God, forgive me. It is yours! All yours!"

Just as we need to be diligent in praising God daily, we need to exercise thanksgiving in all things. Remembering the specific ways God has blessed you and giving thanks each day is a discipline that is important to maintain. It will keep your relationship with God vital and alive. It will lead you to be less anxious about your life and to recognize that God does take care of you. It will help free you to be able to give to others as God has given to you.

Prayers of thanksgiving to God might seem easy when many blessings are flowing to you, but there are those difficult times. Tragedy strikes. Jobs are lost. Sickness prevails. Families are torn apart. Abusive memories haunt. How do you pray then? The New Testament encourages us through both direct admonition and examples of early Christians that we are to pray with thanksgiving in all life's circumstances. 1 Thessalonians 5:18 is very direct in its admonition: "Give thanks in all circumstances; for this is the will of God in Christ Jesus for you." This teaching is echoed in several other New Testament passages:

> *And whatever you do, in word or deed, do everything in the name of the Lord Jesus, giving thanks to God the Father through him.*
>
> *(Colossians 3:17)*

> *Do not worry about anything, but in everything by prayer and supplication with thanksgiving let your requests be made known to God.*
>
> *(Philippians 4:6)*

By giving thanks in all circumstances you give witness that you trust God to act in all situations. This is not to say that God creates our troubles, tragedies, or trials. It does say that God can and will act in the midst of them to create good out of them, as we read in Romans 8:28: "We know that all things work together for good for those who love God, who are called according to his purpose." Prayers of thanksgiving in difficult circumstances give witness to your trust in God's desire and ability to act on your behalf. If you offer a prayer of thanksgiving in the midst of a tragedy, it will help you turn your attention to God, and then you can begin to look with hope for what God might do to redeem and transform the experience.

You have probably experienced the fact that anxiety, anger, or vengeance do not transform life's situations. Even though these feelings are natural and you will experience them, you can begin to discipline yourself to respond to all situations with thanksgiving and move beyond paralyzing or destructive emotions. The writer of Psalm 92 says it best: "It is good to give thanks to the Lord, to sing praises to your name, O Most High; to declare your steadfast love in the morning, and your faithfulness by night" (vv. 1-2). It is good to give thanks to the Lord because that is what God expects from us. God, who freely gives out of grace and in abundance, looks for the grateful heart to respond. It is also good to give thanks because it keeps our spiritual life in balance. It delivers us from anxiety or acting on destructive feelings. Thanksgiving keeps us focused on God's redeeming and transforming possibilities for every situation.

As in other forms of prayer, we see that thanksgiving is a vital discipline in maintaining a healthy relationship with God and in our own spirituality. You may want to develop a pattern or discipline in your own life so that prayers of thanksgiving become a part of your daily routine—giving thanks before each meal; thanking God upon awakening; naming and thanking God each evening for the blessings of the day, and consciously linking each event and person encountered in the day to the ongoing presence of Christ in your life. Forging a habit of gratitude in these obvious situations of blessing and goodness will prepare you to be able to give thanks in the difficult circumstances.

For REFLECTION *and* DISCUSSION

1. What creates a sense of awe and wonder within you? Why do you think this happens? What about God inspires adoration in you? How do you express that awe?

2. What barriers to joy do you detect within yourself? Fear? Shame? Depression? Anxiety? Anger? Have you become accustomed to these negative emotions in your life? Have you become dependent on them as an escape or excuse?

3. When do you pray prayers of thanksgiving? For what things are you most grateful? Reflect on the size of your circle of gratitude. What do you take for granted that is not in the circle?

4. How frequent are your prayers of adoration and praise? Why are these types of prayer important in your prayer life?

ACTIVITIES

1. Choose a psalm verse of praise that you like. Write it on a card and carry it with you. Try to remember to pray that verse each hour of the day.

2. Make a commitment to offer a prayer of praise each morning and evening for thirty days, regardless of how you feel that day. Let your motivation be your commitment. Relate your prayer to a specific aspect of God or God's actions that you have experienced that day. The language of praise is alleluia, honor, glory, blessing, beauty, and holiness. In the beginning your vocabulary of praise might feel limited. Keep at it, focusing on God and God's actions in your life, and you might find your praise time growing longer. After a few days of this exercise, reflect on the way these prayers are affecting your attitudes, emotions, thinking, and relationships. Notice whether or not you are more conscious of God's presence than before. You might want to read Philippians 4:4 before each praise time as an encouragement: "Rejoice in the Lord always; again I will say, Rejoice."

3. For one week, reflect on a portion of Psalm 104. Write in your journal at least five instances of God's footprints in your life each day.

4. Study in depth five psalms of praise. Meditate, then write in your journal about your reflections. Discuss them with others. Read commentaries, Bible dictionaries, and books related to those psalms. Some psalms of praise include 9, 92, 95, 98, 100, 113, 104, 147, and 150.

Chapter Ten

LEARNING *to* PRAY *from* OTHERS

he Christian community is a praying community and a place where you learn from and are sustained by others. The gift and art of prayer have been at the center of this community from the beginning. From the prayers of others you can learn much that will help you make prayer a central part of your life. Be teachable as you journey in prayer.

Learning from the Psalms

This ancient prayer book has accompanied the people of God for centuries. Each generation has found the psalms to be a rich source of learning about prayer. As you read and pray the psalms you will find them speaking about your own life in all its parts, moods, and circumstances.

The psalms will encourage you to be open and honest before God. They are filled with questions about life, God, and oneself. These questions grew out of the life experience of the psalmists as they sought to understand their life situations in the light of God's love and goodness. Notice the openness and intensity of feeling expressed in these questions found in the psalms:

O God, why do you cast us off forever?
Why does your anger smoke against the sheep of your pasture?
(Psalm 74:1)

How long, O Lord? Will you forget me forever?
How long will you hide your face from me?

How long must I bear pain in my soul,
    and have sorrow in my heart all day long?
                    (Psalm 13:1-2)

The psalmists were not afraid to openly express their feelings to God. They did not hide their frustration, anger, fear, or shame. You might be tempted not to allow all your feelings to enter your prayer life. This might come from a false notion that only "nice" things are to be said to God. God knows our lives. God knows our feelings. God is not put off by honesty. In fact, the thing that God desires is truth and sincerity. Whether it is like the serene, pastoral images of Psalm 23 expressing a calm confidence in God's care, or Psalm 137 with its cry for vengeance, prayer is meant to express our true feelings and responses to our life situations.

Truth and sincerity apply to positive as well as to negative emotions. Notice the straightforward expression of confidence and unbridled joy in these psalm verses:

Vindicate me, O Lord,
    for I have walked in my integrity,
    and I have trusted in the Lord without wavering.
Prove me, O Lord, and try me;
    test my heart and mind.
For your steadfast love is before my eyes,
    and I walk in faithfulness to you.
                    (Psalm 26:1-3)

In the prayer conversation with God, the psalms also teach about the inner dialog with your soul. These prayers plumb the depths of the inner journey of prayer. The psalmist's conscious mind speaks to the deeper reality of the soul and calls it into conversation with God:

Why are you cast down, O my soul,
    and why are you disquieted within me?
Hope in God; for I shall again praise him,
    my help and my God.
                    (Psalm 42:5)

Many people find it difficult to define the soul or to talk about it meaning-fully. Because of our cultural emphasis on rationalism and materialism, we tend to discount the nonmaterial and spiritual. A careful reading and reflection on the psalms might help to restore your confidence in the reality of inner, spiritual experience and thus allow your prayer life to blossom. The psalms do not discredit the material and the rational. These aspects of life are fully present in these prayers. However, the psalms also give full expression to the deep soul experience of relating to God.

From the psalms you can also learn about the relationship between prayer and the deep healing of your life. Many of the psalms are prayers of confession and describe the healing experienced when sin is acknowledged and God's mercy is received. Notice in Psalm 32 how the agony and pain of unconfessed sin is relieved when the psalmist confesses:

> *Happy are those whose transgression is forgiven,*
> *whose sin is covered...*
> *While I kept silence, my body wasted away*
> *through my groaning all day long.*
> *For day and night your hand was heavy upon me;*
> *my strength was dried up as by the heat of summer.*
> *Then I acknowledged my sin to you,*
> *and I did not hide my iniquity;*
> *I said, "I will confess my transgressions to the Lord,"*
> *and you forgave the guilt of my sin.*
> *(Psalm 32:1,3-5)*

The deepest need any of us has is for this type of healing in our lives. The guilt, shame, and fear that flow from sin carry such destructive power. Sharing our whole lives with God opens the door for God's grace and mercy to transform us and to restore our wholeness and balance. The psalms point the way for us to pray with complete honesty and humility, trusting with great confidence in the mercy and forgiving love of God. God fulfills and completes this truth with the gift of the Savior, Jesus. The honesty of the psalms, combined with the love of God displayed in the cross of Christ, is an avenue of prayer that can give the deep healing we all need.

Another lesson from the psalms is the encouragement they give us to pray in trust and confidence. The psalmists continuously affirm in their prayers the steadfast love and faithfulness of God. They never tire of reciting the marvelous works of God and the fact that God can be trusted to act now. When you are learning to pray in faith, imitate the psalms by including in your prayers the remembrance of God's mighty deeds. As your prayer grows from remembrances of God's acts, you will be encouraged to pray out of faith and not out of despair over what surrounds you in the world.

Notice the wonderful way the psalmists include praise and adoration in their prayers and confidently affirm God's desire to help and to save. We read for example:

> *O Lord, you will hear the desire of the meek;*
> *   you will strengthen their heart, you will incline your ear*
> *to do justice for the orphan and the oppressed,*
> *   so that those from earth may strike terror no more.*
> *   (Psalm 10:17-18)*

One of the most important lessons of the psalms has to do with the way you see. For the psalmists, God is everywhere. There is no gift but what comes from God. There is no life but what comes from God. There is no rescue but what comes from God. There is no food but what comes from God. This way of seeing undergirds the marvelous prayers in the Book of Psalms. It provides a vision of what our prayer can become. As your prayer life deepens, God will become more present to each moment of your life and more visible in all the signs of life around you. Each moment will carry a metaphor or symbol that can give life and vitality to your conversation with God. Spend some time meditating on Psalm 104 to begin learning how you can begin to see God's footprints and sense God's presence in all of life.

Learning from the Lord's Prayer

In response to his disciples' request to teach them to pray, Jesus gave them the prayer we call the Lord's Prayer. It is a brief but powerful example of prayer that can help us understand how to pray. Some Christians use this prayer several times a day, letting it become the model prayer for their devotional expression to God. It is worth your time to explore this prayer by meditating on its petitions and letting it become a frequent discipline.

Since the Lord's Prayer was given by Jesus, it has a special place in most Christian communities. It is a prayer that will reside deep within your soul and provide a sense—whether conscious or unconscious—of God's presence.

On one occasion I was called to the hospital to minister to an elderly person who was dying. She was in a coma when I arrived and had been unresponsive to the communication of family and nursing staff. I spoke to the woman about God's redemptive love in Jesus and prayed for her. Then I began praying the Lord's Prayer. By the third sentence of the prayer I noticed her lips moving in unison with the words I was saying. Even though she made no sound, from deep within, where the prayer had become implanted in her soul, she was responding and participating in this conversation with God. It is wonderful to have the truth of this prayer planted deep within us. It can be an unconscious yet real prayer that continues, even when the conscious mind is asleep.

The Lord's Prayer is a good teacher about prayer because it is so simple and direct. It acknowledges God as One who is beyond us and yet is a tenderhearted and compassionate Father. It further praises God by holding up the holiness of God's name. God's kingdom—that is, God's rule and will in our world—is requested. Then follow requests for three basic needs in our life: for daily food, receiving and giving forgiveness, and protection from evil. This fundamental prayer teaches us to honor God, open our lives to God's will, and live without anxiety and fear by trusting God to supply our daily needs, forgive us, and protect us from evil.

Learning from Classic Prayers

In the Christian community we learn from each other. The wisdom of Christians, past and present, is a continuous source of wealth. This is true of prayer as well as other aspects of religious life. You can gain inspiration and insight from the prayers handed down through the centuries. These prayers have been a wellspring of encouragement and learning for Christians all over the world. Often they provide ways of praying with creativity and sensitivity when our own well is dry and our spirit is lagging. You might find it helpful to use these prayers as a way to find your own voice in prayer. The creative style and the wise content can be a teacher for your own prayer journey with God.

Following are some prayer classics that have fed countless numbers of people.

> *God grant me the serenity*
> *To accept the things that I cannot change,*
> *The courage to change the things I can,*
> *And the wisdom to know the difference.*
> *—Reinhold Niebuhr*

> *Most merciful Redeemer, Friend, and Brother, may we know Thee more clearly,*
> *love Thee more dearly, and follow Thee more nearly: for Thine own sake. Amen.*
> *—Richard of Chichester*

God, give us grateful hearts. For if we do not have the grace to thank Thee for
all that we have and enjoy, how can we have the effrontery to seek Thy further
blessing? For Jesus sake. Amen.   —*Peter Marshall*[1]

Thou hast given so much to me,
Give one thing more—a grateful heart;
Not thankful when it pleases me,
As if Thy blessings had spare days,
But such a heart whose pulse may be
Thy praise.
                              —*George Herbert*[2]

O Lord, the sea is so large and my boat is so small.
Have mercy and help me. Amen.
                              —*Celtic Prayer*

Come Holy Spirit. Fill the hearts of your faithful, and kindle in us the fire of your
love. Send forth your Spirit and we shall be created and you shall renew the face
of the earth. O God, who by the light of your Holy Spirit did instruct the hearts of
the faithful, grant that by that same Spirit we may be truly wise and ever enjoy
his consolations. Through Christ our Lord. Amen.
                              —*Adapted from the psalms and ancient collects*

Learning from Hymns and Liturgy

Most hymns are prayers set to music. They express praise, thanksgiving,
desire, and grief. These poetic texts are another source of learning about prayer.
Augustine said, "To sing is to pray twice." Combining music and poetry
involves more dimensions of yourself in the act of praying. Music helps to draw
out the emotions of the heart and lets our thoughts, body, and feelings join
together in prayer.

Begin to think of singing hymns and spiritual songs as an act of prayer,
whether you sing alone or with others. Discover how your singing changes
when you think of it as prayer. Forget about what your voice sounds like and let
your whole self join in this prayer experience. God is interested that you pray,
not in how you sound when you pray. God is listening to the heart-cry of your
prayer, not to the quality of your voice.

The liturgy of your church can function in the same way. It gives one voice to the people of God gathered for prayer. However, the language and song of the liturgy can also be the prayer of one voice. These ancient and abiding prayers of the church can become the vehicle for a rich prayer life, whether alone or with others.

You are not alone in your prayer journey. Thousands have journeyed before and thousands journey with you today. Enrich your prayer life from the collected wisdom and devotion of your brothers and sisters in the faith. Scripture, hymns, liturgy, the prayers of others—all these are resources that will assist you in learning to pray.

For REFLECTION *and* DISCUSSION

1. Are you offended by certain styles of prayer? What are they and why do they offend you? What are the characteristics of your style of prayer?

2. Think about your favorite hymns. Do they have a common theme or mood? Is the focus of your prayers similar to that of your favorite hymns? How have your prayers been influenced by the hymns and liturgies with which you grew up?

3. How do you understand the role of public prayer—joining with others in following the prayers of a worship leader? Do you struggle with praying in the corporate worship setting? What distracts you during this time?

4. Who has taught you the most about prayer? What significant knowledge about prayer have you received from others?

ACTIVITIES

1. Reflect on your prayer journey. Make a list of people who have influenced both your desire to pray and how you pray. What inspired you about each person and what did you learn from them?

2. Compare Psalms 38, 96, and 121. What mood dominates each psalm? What moments in your life are similar to the situations in the psalms? Does the psalm help you discover a way to pray in those situations?

3. For one week, practice a daily morning and evening reading of the psalms. Begin with Psalm 1 and read them in succession. As you read through the week, notice what you are learning about prayer. You might want to write your insights in your prayer journal.

4. The Lord's Prayer has been called the model prayer. Set aside a quiet day to focus your attention on this prayer. Spend time meditating on each phrase. Apply each phrase to your life, seeing what direction it gives you about your attitudes, expectations, and practice of prayer. After your meditation, rewrite the prayer in your own words as you have come to understand it through your reflection.

5. Attend a worship service and consciously pray in and through every part of the service. Prepare for this visit by examining the service and noting what kind of prayer is involved in various parts of the worship: silence, confession, meditation on the Word, praise, thanksgiving, intercessions, and cries for mercy. Notice the changes in mood, posture, style of praying, and focus. Afterward, discuss with others what you learned and compare their experience with yours. You might want to repeat this often as a way to grow in your prayer life.

6. Begin to memorize prayers others have written that are meaningful to you and that speak your heart's desire.

1. Donald Kauffman, ed., *A Treasury of Great Prayers* (Westwood, N.J.: Fleming H. Revell, 1964), p. 23.

2. Ibid. p. 41.

Chapter Eleven

PRAYER *and* LIFE'S JOURNEY

erhaps your prayer life began when as a small child
you spoke these words as you went to bed:

Now I lay me down to sleep.
I pray the Lord my soul to keep.
If I should die before I wake,
I pray the Lord my soul to take.

And at the end of life, the prayer often echoes Jesus' last words on the
cross: "Father, into your hands I commend my spirit."

Moving full circle from birth to death, life is enfolded with the knowledge
and the prayer that we receive life as a gift and offer with thanksgiving it back
to God.

In between these simple bookends of prayer, life is filled with the struggle
to know ourselves, others, and God, and with all the decisions that grow out of
this knowledge. What should I do with my life? What is important and of
value? With whom should I live my life? We encounter change along life's journey from childhood to youth, to young adulthood, to mid-life, and then to
older adulthood. Each change brings new experiences and challenges. Life is
like a school that continually tests us through new tasks. Each stage brings a
challenge to our faith, character, hope, strength, and love. We will encounter
great joy and great sorrow, success and failure, love and rejection.

In, with, and under this journey is the ongoing presence of our Lord. God
is there in the midst of all that life brings. Prayer is the opportunity to relate
your life journey to that ever-present reality of God's promise to love you and

keep you forever. For this reason, the ultimate test is to remain faithful to God as God has promised to be faithful to you. Your faithfulness can be nurtured through your commitment to pray, so that your successes can be met with humility and your disappointments with hope. Prayer will help you live with the knowledge that God has bread enough for the journey. God is present in each day with what it takes to nourish and sustain your life. The well of God's abundant grace never runs dry.

Prayer is not a journey of self-actualization during which you realize that you don't need God. Rather, prayer is a journey of discovery and you are being held in the palm of God's hand at every stage. A commitment to the discipline of prayer within yourself and with others will keep you close to God's saving and nurturing grace in Christ Jesus. As the apostle Paul heard from the Lord, "My grace is sufficient for you" (2 Corinthians 12:9). So you can depend on that promise for your life.

Following are thoughts that might help you develop and maintain a healthy discipline of prayer:

- Seek God first in all things. Remember that the foundation for prayer is the relationship you have with God.
- Maintain a regular discipline of prayer. Find the way that is best for you to keep prayer at the center of your religious life. "Commit your way to the Lord; trust in him, and he will act" (Psalm 37:5).
- Pray, trusting in God's love for you. Center your prayer in the cross and resurrection of Jesus, where God has displayed that wondrous love for you.
- Give thanks in everything. Learn the power of gratitude and praise to transform your responses to life's situations.
- Follow God's lead in prayer. The Holy Spirit is the great teacher of prayer. Learn to discern the inner movement of God's Spirit in your soul.
- Expect to grow spiritually through your prayer discipline. Maturity will come in the enlightenment and wisdom God will bring to your life.
- Expect to be surprised. God, at times, will do more than you expect or can imagine.
- Offer God everything. Whatever you hold back for your own control can become a barrier to clarity in discerning God's will.
- Be honest in sharing with God.
- Listen, listen, listen.

All of life and all of prayer is a journey of return to the One who has made you, the One who waits eagerly for you with these words of invitation:

I am the Alpha and the Omega, the beginning and the end. To the thirsty I will give water as a gift from the spring of the water of life. Those who conquer will inherit these things, and I will be their God and they will be my children.
(Revelation 21:6-7)

"Now I lay me down to sleep," "Father, into your hands I commend my spirit," and all the prayers in between are part of this marvelous journey with God that ends in God.

For REFLECTION *and* DISCUSSION

1. How has your understanding and practice of prayer changed as you have moved through different life stages? Look again at the chart you prepared at the beginning of this book. Are there things to add? Things to change?

2. What obstacles have you overcome through your study of prayer? What obstacles remain?

3. In this study of prayer, what is the most helpful lesson you have learned ?

ACTIVITIES

1. Write your current definition of prayer. Compare it with the definition you wrote at the end of the introduction. How has it changed?

2. Write down what you believe is the best type of prayer discipline for you to follow. What areas of prayer do you want to explore more deeply? Can you think of a next step for your growth? What, for you, is the biggest unanswered question about prayer?

3. Write a brief description of how your relationship with God has changed through this study of prayer.

FOR FURTHER READING

Anonymous. *The Cloud of Unknowing.* New York: Image Books, 1973.

Bloom, Anthony. *Beginning to Pray.* New York: Paulist Press, 1979.

Brother Lawrence. *The Practice of the Presence of God.* Old Tappen, N.J.: Revell, 1958.

Egan, Harvey D. *Christian Mysticism.* New York: Pueblo, 1984.

Foster, Richard J. *Prayer.* San Francisco: Harper, 1992.

Hallesby, O. *Prayer.* Minneapolis: Augsburg Books, 1993 (1931).

Kelsey, Morton T. *The Other Side of Silence.* New York: Paulist Press, 1976.

Klug, Ron. *How to Keep a Spiritual Journal.* Minneapolis: Augsburg Books, 1994.

Michael, Chester D., and Marie C. Norrisey. *Prayer and Temperament.* Charlottesville, Va.: The Open Door Inc., 1984.

Pennington, M. Basil. *Centering Prayer.* New York: Image Books, 1980.

Sager, Allan H. *Gospel-Centered Spirituality.* Minneapolis: Augsburg Books, 1990.

Teresa of Avila, *The Interior Castle.* New York: Paulist Press, 1979.

Look for these other titles in

Face to Face with God: A Guide for Prayer Ministry

Coming Face to Face with God: Conversations on Prayer (video)
Seeking God's Face: A Prayer Journal

Readers for individual or group use:

Prayer for Friends and Enemies: Intercessory Prayer
Praying for Wholeness and Healing

Handbooks for pastors and other church leaders:

Face to Face with God in Your Church: Establishing a Prayer Ministry
Face to Face with God in Your Home: Guiding Children and Youth in Prayer